BASIC PRINCIPLES

OF

ORGANIC CHEMISTRY

Sanjeev Jena

Lecturer
Department of Chemistry
Jyoti English Medium Higher Secondary School
Charoda Durg CG India

Dr. Vinod Jena

Assistant Professor
Department of Chemistry
Government College Sarona Kanker CG India

2015

First Printing: 2015

ISBN: 978-1-312-78297-6

DEDICATION

To my friends all over the world.

Thank you all.

Without your support and patience, I would have never achieved my

dream.

ACKNOWLEDGMENTS

I would like to thank my teachers, my editor, my classmates, and my family without whose help this book would never have been completed.

CONTENTS

CHAPTER 1

COVALENT BOND CLEAVAGE

Covalent bond cleavage

A **covalent bond** is a chemical **bond** that involves the sharing of electron pairs between atoms. The stable balance of attractive and repulsive forces between atoms when they share electrons is known as **covalent bonding**.

Breaking of covalent bond of the compound is known as **bond fission**. A bond can be broken by two ways,

Homolytic bond fission or Homolysis

In homolysis, the covalent bond is broken in such a way that each resulting species gets its own electron. This leads to the formation of odd electron species known as **free radical**.

$$A:B \longrightarrow \overset{\bullet}{A} + \overset{\bullet}{B}$$
Free Radical

(ii) The factor which favours homolysis is that the difference in electronegativity between and is less or zero.

(iii) Homolysis takes place in gaseous phase or in the presence of non polar solvents (CCl_4, CS_2), peroxide, ($\geq 500°C$) light, heat, electricity and free radical.

(iv) Mechanism of the reaction in which homolysis takes place is known as homolytic mechanism or free radical mechanism.

2) Heterolytic bond fission or heterolysis

(i) In heterolysis, the covalent bond is broken in such a way that one species (*i.e.*, less electronegative) is deprived of its own electron, while the other species gains both the electrons.

$$A:B \longrightarrow A^- \quad + \quad B^+$$

$$\text{Carboanion} \qquad \text{Carocation}$$

Thus formation of opposite charged species takes place. In case of organic compounds, if positive charge is present on the carbon then cation is termed as **carbocation**. If negative charge is present on the carbon then anion is termed as **carbanion**.

(i) The factor which favours heterolysis is greater difference of electronegativities between and

(ii) Mechanism of the reaction in which heterolysis takes place is known as heterolytic mechanism or ionic mechanism.

(iii) The energy required for heterolysis is always greater than that for homolysis due to electrostatic forces of attraction between ions.

CHAPTER 2

Attacking Reagents

Most of the attacking reagents can be classified into two main groups.

Electrophiles or electrophilic reagents and Nucleophiles or nucleophilic reagents.

(1) Electrophiles: Electron deficient species or electron acceptor is an electrophile.

It can be classified into two categories:

(i) Charged electrophiles: Positively charged species in which central atom has incomplete octet is called charged electrophile.

$$H^+, \ X^+, \ R^+, \ NO_2^+, \ SO_3H^+,$$

All cations are charged electrophiles except cations of IA, IIA group elements, Al^{+++} and NH_4^+

(ii) Neutral electrophiles : It can be classified into three categories,

(a) Neutral covalent compound in which central atom has incomplete octet is neutral electrophile,

$$BeCl_2, \ BH_3, \ ZnCl_2, \ AlX_3, \ FeX_3, \ \overset{\centerdot}{C}H_3, \ \overset{\centerdot\centerdot}{C}H_2, \ \overset{\centerdot\centerdot}{C}X_2$$

(b) Neutral covalent compound in which central atom has complete or expended octet and central atom has unfilled –d-sub-shell is neutral electrophile,

$$SnCl_4, \ SiCl_4, \ PCl_5, \ SF_6, \ IF_7$$

(c) Neutral covalent compound in which central atom is bonded only with two or more than two electronegative atoms is called neutral electrophile.

$BeCl_2$, BX_3, AlX_3, FeX_3, $SnCl_4$, PCl_3;

$P\overset{..}{C}l_5$, NF_3, CX_2, CO_2, SO_3, CS_2, Cl_2, Br_2 and I_2 and also behave as neutral electrophiles.

Electrophiles are Lewis acids.

(2) Nucleophiles : Electron rich species or electron donors are called nucleophiles. Nucleophiles can be classified into three categories :

(i) Charged nucleophiles: Negatively charged species are called charged nucleophiles.

H^-, OH^-, $R - O^-$, CH_3^-, X^-, $S- H^-$, $R - S^-$

(ii) Neutral nucleophiles : It can be classified into two categories :

 (a) Neutral covalent compound, in which central atom has complete octet, has at least one lone pair of electrons and all atoms present on central atom should not be electronegative, is neutral nucleophile.

$\overset{..}{N}H_3$, $R-\overset{..}{N}H_2$, $R_2\overset{..}{N}H$, $R_3\overset{..}{N}$, NH_2-NH_2 (Nitrogen nucleophile)

$$H - \overset{..}{\underset{..}{O}} - H, R - \overset{..}{\underset{..}{O}} - H, R - \overset{..}{\underset{..}{O}} - R \text{ (Oxygen nucleophiles)}$$

$$H - \overset{..}{\underset{..}{S}} - H, R - \overset{..}{\underset{..}{S}} - H, R - \overset{..}{\underset{..}{S}} - R \text{ (Sulphur nucleophiles)}$$

$$\overset{..}{P} H_3, R - \overset{..}{P} - H_2, R - \overset{..}{P} - H, R_{3-} \overset{..}{P} \text{ (Phosphorus nucleophiles)}$$

(b) Organic compound containing carbon, carbon multiple bond/ bonds behaves as nucleophile.

Alkenes, Alkynes, Benzene,

$$CH_2 = CH - CH = CH_2, CH_2 = CH - C \equiv CH$$

(iii) Ambident nucleophiles : Species having two nucleophilic centres out of which, one is neutral (complete octet and has at least one lone pair of electrons) and the other is charged (negative charge) behaves as ambident nucleophile

$$C = N, O - N = O, O - S - OH$$
$$\downarrow$$

O

- Organometallic compounds are nucleophiles.
- Nucleophiles are Lewis bases.

Organic compounds which behave as an electrophile as well as a nucleophile : Organic compound in which carbon is bonded with electronegative atom (O, N, S) by multiple bond/bonds behaves as electrophile as well as nucleophile:

$$\overset{O}{\overset{\|}{R-C-H}}, \quad \overset{O}{\overset{\|}{R-C-R}}, \quad \overset{O}{\overset{\|}{R-C-OH}}, \quad \overset{O}{\overset{\|}{R-C-NH_2}}$$

$$R - C = N, R - N = C \qquad \text{etc.}$$

CHAPTER 3

ELECTRON DISPLACEMENTS IN ORGANIC MOLECULES

In organic molecules different reactions depend on the electron density in their molecules. Since majority of attacking reagents are polar, i.e. nucleophilic (or) electrophilic, hence in organic compounds permanent (or) temporary polarity is developed by temporary (or) permanent electron displacements.The following four types of electronic effects operates in covalent bonds

- Inductive effect
- Mesomeric and Resonance effect
- Electronic effects
- Hyperconjugation

Electron displacement is of two types:

Permanent effects: (i) Inductive effect(ii) Mesomeric effect

Temporary Effect (i) Electromeric Effect (ii) Inductomeric Effect

1. Inductive effect

In a covalent bond between the two dissimilar atoms, the electron pair forming the bond is never shared absolutely equally between the two atoms but is attracted a little more towards the more electronegative atom of the two, eg. The electron pair forming the C–

X bond is somewhat more attracted towards the atom X with the result – it attains a partial negative charge $(-\delta)$ while the carbon atoms attain a partial positive charge $(+\delta)$

$$C:X \text{ or } \overset{\delta^+}{C}-\overset{\delta^-}{X}$$

On the other hand, in compounds like C–Y, where Y in an electropositive element or group i.e., C is more electronegative than Y, the electron pair forming the C–Y bond is somewhat displaced towards the carbon atom and thus C and Y attain partial negative and partial positively charges respectively.

$$C: Y \text{ or } \overset{\delta^-}{C}-\overset{\delta^+}{Y}$$

According to Ingold sign convention, the former is called as $(-I)$ effect and the later is called as $(+I)$ effect.

The inductive effect is represented by the symbol $\rightarrow$, the arrow pointing towards the more electronegative element or group of elements eg. N – butyl chloride .

$$\overset{\delta\delta\delta\delta^+}{CH_3} \rightarrow \overset{\delta\delta\delta^+}{CH_2} \rightarrow \overset{\delta\delta^+}{CH_2} \rightarrow \overset{\delta^+}{CH_2} \rightarrow \overset{-\delta-}{Cl}$$

The extent of positive charge keeps on decreasing away from Cl atom and at third and fourth carbon it is almost zero for all practical purposes.

Examples of Inductive effect:

(–I) effect group (electron attracting)

$$\overset{+}{N}Me_3 > \overset{+}{N}H_3 > NO_2 > CN > COOH > F > Cl > Br > I > OAr > COOR > OR > OH$$
$$> C_6H_5 > CH = CH_2 > H$$

(+I) effect – group (electron– repelling)

$$C_6H_5O^- > COO^- > R_3C > CHR_2 > CH_2R > CH_3 > H$$

Applications of Inductive Effect

(i) Dipole moment: Since, inductive effect leads to a dipolar character in the molecule, it develops some dipole moment in the molecule, which increases with the increase in the inductive effect.

$$CH_3 \longrightarrow I \quad CH_3 \longrightarrow Br \quad CH_3 \longrightarrow Cl$$
$$1.648D \quad\quad\quad 1.79D \quad\quad\quad 1.83D$$

Increasing   dipole moment

_(ii)   In Bond Length: With increase in inductive effect, the bond length usually decreases because of increased ionic character,

$$CH_3 \longrightarrow F \quad CH_3 \longrightarrow Cl \quad CH_3 \longrightarrow Br \quad CH_3 \longrightarrow I$$
$$1.38Å \qquad\quad 1.78Å \qquad\quad 1.94Å \qquad\quad 2.14Å$$

(iii) Strength of Fatty Acids: As the number of alkyl groups attached to –COOH group increases, the acid strength decreases. Thus formic acid is stronger acid than acetic acid which is stronger than propionic acid and so on, due to increasing +I effect of alkyl groups.

(Formic acid)   (Acetic acid)   (Propanoic acid)

(iv)   Strength of Substituted Acids: Chlorinated acetic acids are stronger than acetic acid due to the – I effect of chlorine atom.

Larger the number of chlorine atoms, the greater will be –I and the stronger will be the acid.

The relative strength of the different halogen substituted acids is

FCH2COOH > ClCH2COOH > BrCH2COOH >

ICH2COOH

(v)   Reactivity of Alkyl Halides: The carbon-halogen bond in tertiary alkyl halides is most reactive while it is least reactive in primary alkyl halides. This can be explained on the basis of greater + I effect in t-alkyl halides which pushes the – I effect; hence the bond becomes   highly   polar   and   most   weak.

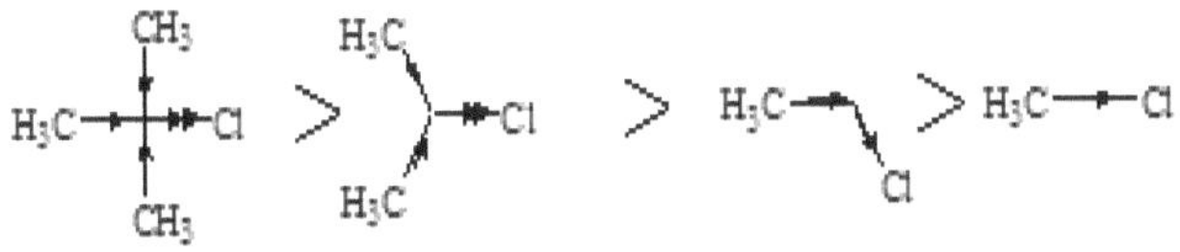

Strength of Carboxylic Acids: Strength of an acid depends upon the ease with which an acid ionises to give proton. A molecule of carboxylic acid can be represented as a resonance hybrid of the following structures.

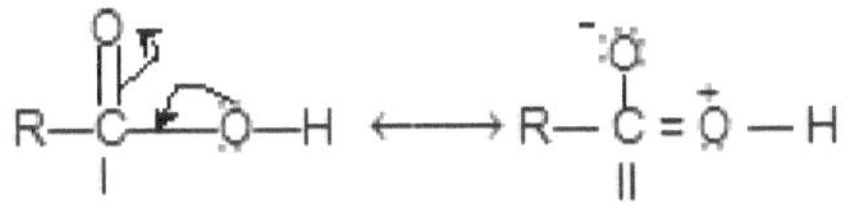

In the II structure, the oxygen atom of the hydroxyl group has a positive charge due to which it has a tendency to attract electron pair (inductive effect) of the O—H bond towards itself, which results in the removal of hydrogen atom as proton and hence carboxylic acids behave as acids.

Once, the carboxylate anion is formed, it is stabilised more easily by resonance than undissociated acid.

Thus, the acidity of carboxylic acid is due to inductive effect and resonance stabilisation of the carboxylate anion. Thus any group or atom, which is highly electronegative help in removing the hydrogen atom as proton and the group or atom which is less electronegative than C makes the removal of proton difficult. Hence (–I) effect group increases acidic strength and (+I) effect groups decreases the acidic strength of carboxylic acid.

Basic strength of Amines : The basic character of amines is due to presence of unshared electron pair on nitrogen atom which accepts proton; the readiness with which the lone pair of electrons available for protonotion determines the relative strength of amines.Due to +I effect of alkyl group, the nitrogen atom becomes rich in electrons with the result the lone pair of electron on nitrogen atom in amines is more easily available than in ammonia and hence generally, amines are stronger bases than ammonia. On the other (–I) groups or electron groups attached to nitrogen atom makes it difficult for protonation.

Mesomeric and Resonance effect

There are many organic molecules which cannot be represented by a single lewis structure. In turn, they are assigned more than one structure called canonical forms or contributing of resonating structures. The phenomenon exhibited by such compounds is called resonance. For example, 1, 3 – butadiene has following resonance structure.

$$H_2C=CH-CH=CH_2 \longleftrightarrow H_2C^{\oplus}-CH=CH-\overset{\ominus}{C}H_2 \longleftrightarrow \overset{\ominus}{H_2C}-CH=CH-$$

and canonical forms of vinyl chloride are

$$H_2C=CH-\ddot{C}l \longleftrightarrow H_2\overset{\ominus}{C}-CH=\overset{\oplus}{C}l$$

While drawing these canonical forms, the prime thing that has to be kept in mind is that the relative position of any of the atom should not change while we are allowed to change the relative positions of p - bonded electron pair or distribution of charge to other atoms.

The conditions necessary for a compound to show resonance. The two essential conditions are

There must be conjugation in the molecule. Conjugation is defined as the presence of alternate double and single bonds in the compound

like

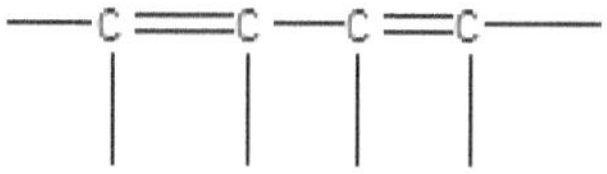

$$-C=C-C=C-$$

The part of the molecules having conjugation must be essentially planar or nearly planar. The first condition of conjugation is not only confined to the one mentioned above but some other systems are also categorized under conjugation. These are

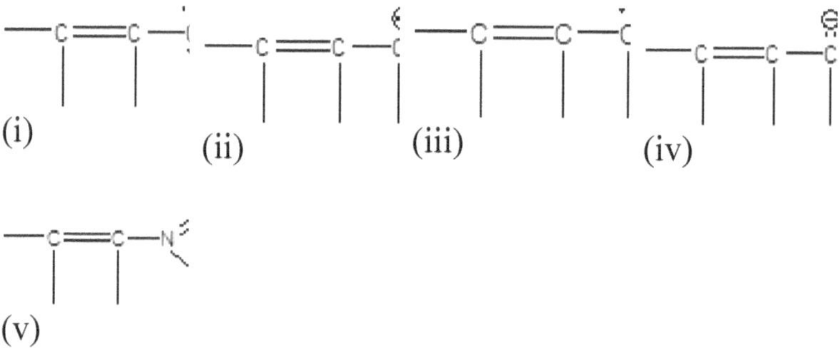

$$-C=C-\overset{.}{\underset{}{C}} \quad -C=C-\overset{.}{\underset{}{C}} \quad -C=C-\overset{.}{\underset{}{C}} \quad -C=C-\overset{\ominus}{\underset{}{C}}$$

(i)   (ii)   (iii)   (iv)

$$-C=C-N$$

(v)

So, any molecules satisfying both the conditions will show resonance. For example, we consider phenol. The structure of phenol is

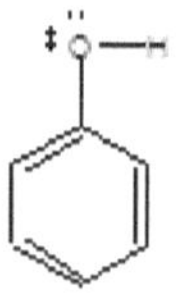

By looking at the structure, it must be clear to you that the compound possesses conjugation of the type

As well as the category (i) because the lone pairs on oxygen are in conjugation with unsaturated (sp2 hybridised) carbon of the ring. Since, oxygen atom is sp3 hybridized in phenol.

The lone pairs on oxygen are nearly planar with respect to the PZ orbital of carbon linked to oxygen. Thus, both the conditions are fulfilled by phenol, therefore it does show resonance.

Resonance always results in different distribution of electron density than would be the case if there were no resonance. It is a permanent effect, also referred as mesomeric effect.

The acidity of phenol can be explained by resonance

Phenol   Penoxide ion

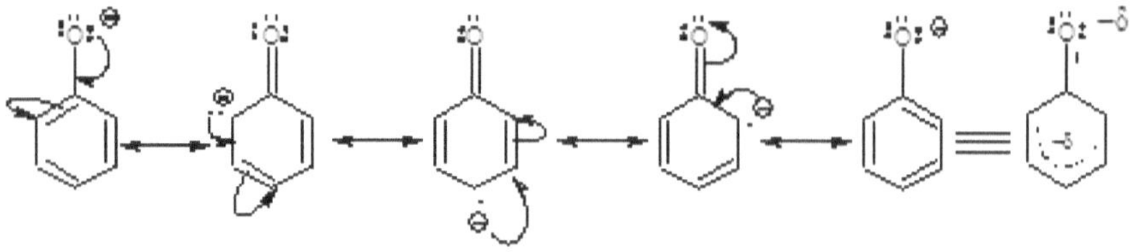

The above structure shows that the phenoxide ion formed is more resonance stabilised than phenol. Hence, the acidity of phenol

Similarly basicity of aniline can be explained.

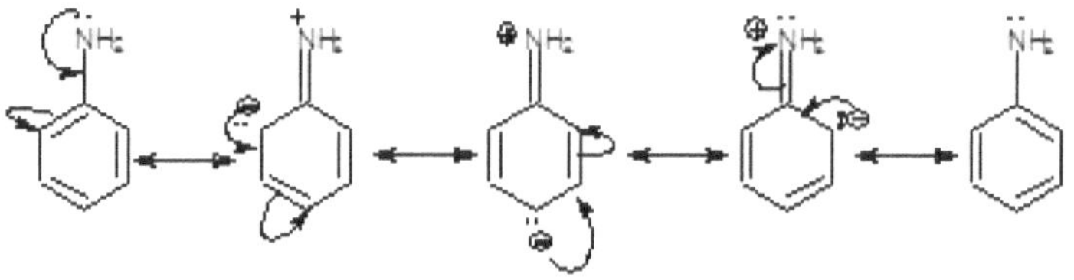

The above structure shows that the lone pair present on N – atom undergoes into resonance and is not available for donation. Hence, the basicity of aniline decreases and is less than aliphatic amine

$$R - \overset{\cdot\cdot}{N}H_2$$

Resonance (mesomeric) effect is of two types.

(i) If the atom or group of atoms is giving electrons through resonance, it is called +R or +M effect. For example,

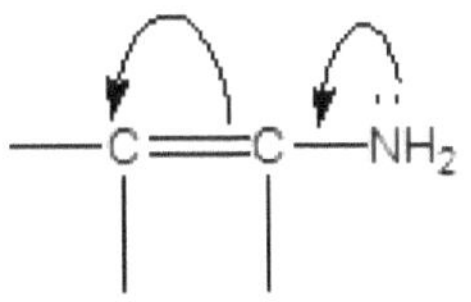

(+M effect of -NH$_2$ group)

Other groups that shows +M effect are -NHR, -NR$_2$, -OH, -OR, -NHCOR, -Cl, -Br,-I etc.

ii) If the atom or group of atoms is withdrawing electrons through resonance, it is called +R or +M effect. For example,

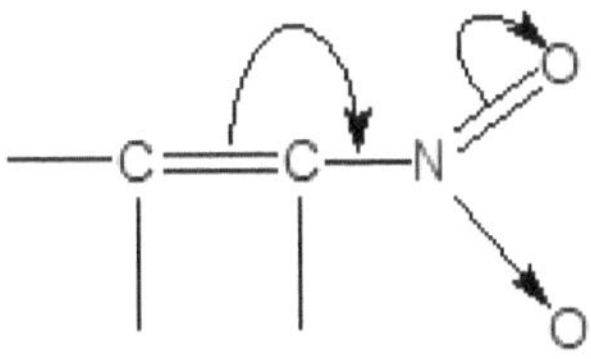

(-M effect of -NO$_2$ group)

Other groups showing -M effect are -CN, -CHO, -COR, -CO$_2$H, -CO$_2$R, -CONH$_2$, -SO$_3$H, -COCl etc.

nitrobenzene

Effect of Resonance

Dipole moment: Dipole moment of certain compounds can be explained by resonance eg. Vinylchloride

$$CH_2 = CH - Cl \longleftrightarrow H_2\bar{C} - CH = \overset{+}{Cl}$$
$$\mu = 1.4D$$

Bond length: the phenomenon of resonance explain the abnormal bond length between C—C, C = C, C = O, etc in compounds exhibiting resonance e.g. in benzene C—C bond length acquires a value which lies between C—C single bond length (1.54Å) and C = C (double bond) length (1.33Å)

Strength of acids and bases: The concept of resonance explain clearly the acidic character of acids and basic character of bases eg. resonance explains why the alcohols are neutral and carboxylic acids are strong acids.

$$ROH \rightleftharpoons RO^- + H^+$$

$$R-C\underset{OH}{\overset{O}{\rightleftharpoons}} \rightleftharpoons R-C\underset{O^-}{\overset{O}{\diagdown}} + H^+$$

But after loss of H+ carboxylate ion R-COO- undergo resonance and stabilised, hence it will favour the loss of H+ ions

Contribution of Resonating structures:

The contribution of an individual factors:

(i)   Neutral species is more stable than the charged (or dipolar spices).

(ii)   Species having complete octet is more stable than the species having incomplete octet

$$R-\overset{\oplus}{C}=\ddot{O} \qquad R-C\equiv\overset{..}{O}$$
$$\;\;\;\;e=6\;\;e=8 \qquad\quad e=8\;\;e=8$$
$$\qquad (I) \qquad\qquad\qquad (II)$$

(I)   and (II) are resonating structure of acyl cation. (II) will be
        more sable than (I).

(iii) If all structure have formal charge, the most stable one is that in which the positive and negative charges reside on the most electropositive and most electronegative atoms of the species respectively.

$$\underset{I}{H-\underset{\overset{|}{O^{\ominus}}}{\overset{|}{C}}-OH} \qquad \underset{II}{H-\underset{\overset{|}{O^{\ominus}}}{\overset{|}{C}}-OH}$$

(iv)   Resonating structure with a greater number of covalent bonds is more stable.

(v)   increase in charge separation decreases the stability of a resonating structure.

(I)   (II)   (III)   (IV)

Hence stability of II and IV will be the same and both will be more stable than III. The order of stability of resonating structures in decreasing order will be as follows:

$$I > II ° IV > III$$

Note : All the resonating structure do not contribute equally to the real molecule . Their contribution is a direct function of their stability.

Resonance and Bond order :

Bond order in conjugated compound or bond order in compounds which exhibit resonance =

$$\frac{\text{Total number of bonds on central atom}}{\text{Number of resonating structures}}$$

Bond order of carbon in benzene = = 1.5

Steric Inhibition of Resonance:

The most important condition for resonance to occur is that the involved atoms in resonating structure must be coplanar or nearly coplanar for maximum resonance. If this condition does not fulfill, the involved orbitals cannot be parallel to each other and as a consequence delocalisation of electrons or positive charge cannot occur. The planarity of orbitals are inhibited by the bulky groups present on adjacent atoms. This phenomenon is known as steric inhibition of resonance. For example, in dimethyl aniline (I) the orbital having lone pair of electrons present on nitrogen atom is in the plane of the benzene hence lone pair of electrons present on nitrogen atom is in the plane of the benzene ring hence lone pair takes part in the delocalisation.

In N, N-dimethyl-2, 6-dinitroaniline (II) the (CH3)2 groups is out of the plane of the benzene ring owing to the presence of the two bulky nitro groups and consequently the lone pair of electrons on the nitrogen atoms of (CH3)2 group cannot get delocalised through lone pair, p conjugation.

 Thus bulky groups present at ortho position inhibit delocalisation of lone pair of electrons or positive charge present on key atom of the molecule. Steric inhibition of resonance has profound effect on:

   (i)   Physical properties   (ii)   Acidity and Basicity   and
   (iii)   Reactivity of organic compounds

In nitro-benzene (I) bond length between carbon-nitrogen (bond -a) is in between single and double due to the resonance but in compound (II) bond length between carbon-nitrogen is only of single bond due to the inhibition of resonance.

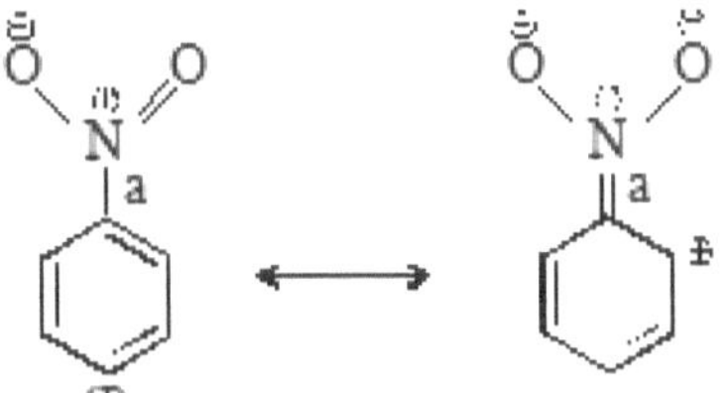

(I)

(II)

Two further points should be noted. First, bond strength is dependent on the extent of the overlap of the combining atomic orbitals, so that in these conjugated systems the more nearly equal in size the p-orbitals are, the more effective is the -orbital overlap. Hence fluorine is more effective than chlorine in conjugating with carbon, and oxygen is more effective than sulphur . Hence the order of + M effects is :

+ M effect possessing groups are:

$$-\ddot{O}H, -\ddot{O}R, -\ddot{N}H_2, -\ddot{N}HR, -\ddot{N}R_2, -\ddot{S}R, -\ddot{X}$$ etc.

– M effect possessing groups are:

—CHO, = CO, — CN, — NO$_2$, — SO$_3$H etc.

Electromeric effects

It is a temporary effect in which a shared pair of electron (p - electron pair) is completely transferred from a double bond or triple bond to one of the atoms joined by the bond at the requirement of attacking reagent.

$$\overset{}{\underset{\text{agent}}{\xrightarrow{\text{Attacking}}}}$$

>C=O $\xrightarrow[\text{agent}]{\text{Attacking}}$ >$\overset{+}{C}$--O^{-}

Case 1:   When multiple bond is present between two similar atom (symmetric alkenes or alkynes) electronic shift can take place in any direction

$$CH_2 = CH_2 \overset{HBr}{\to} CH_2^- = CH_2^+$$

Note 1:   If two carbon atoms are different (asymmetric alkenes or alkynes) then the direction of electronic shift is determined by the direction of the inductive effect of the group present at doubly or triply bonded atom e.g.,.

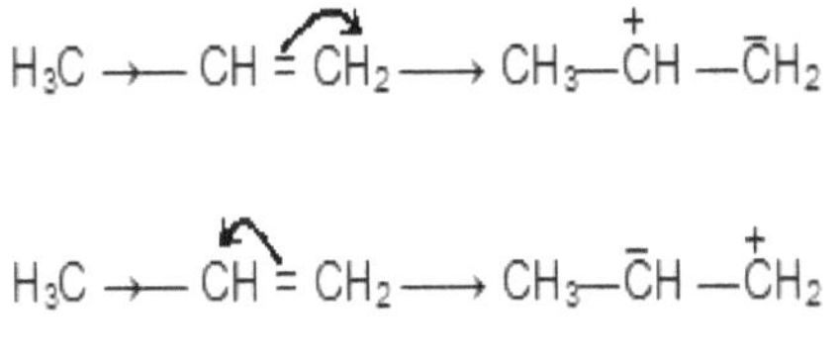

$H_3C \longrightarrow CH = CH_2 \longrightarrow CH_3 - CH - \overset{+}{C}H_2$ (Favoured by +I effect)

$H_3C \longrightarrow CH = CH_2 \longrightarrow CH_3 - \overset{-}{C}H - \overset{+}{C}H_2$ (Opposite shift is not possible because it will be opposed by +I – effect)

Note 2: When inductive and electromeric effects oppose each other, in such cases, electromeric effect usually overcome inductive effect eg.

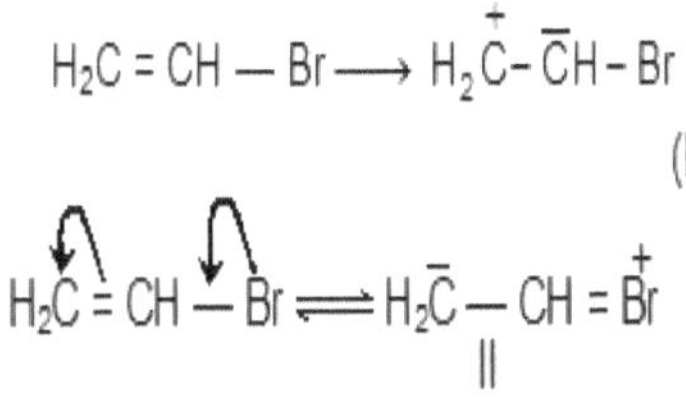

$H_2C = CH - Br \longrightarrow H_2\overset{+}{C} - \overset{-}{C}H - Br$ (E-effect operate in the direction of I-effect)

(I)

$H_2C = CH - Br \rightleftharpoons H_2\overset{-}{C} - CH = \overset{+}{Br}$ (E-effect operate opposite to I-effect)

II

Types of Electromeric Effects:

+E Effect: The electron of pi bond are transferred to that atom of the double bond to which the reagent gets finally attached. For example:

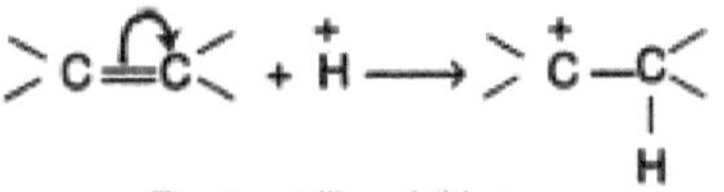

$>C = C< + \overset{+}{H} \longrightarrow > \overset{-}{C} - \overset{+}{C} <$ (+ E effect)

Electrophilic addition

–E effect: The electron of pi bond are transferred to that atom of the double bond other than the one to which the reagent gets finally

31

attached. For example:

$$\underset{\text{Nucleophilic addition}}{\overset{\displaystyle >}{C} = \overset{\cdot\cdot}{O}: \overset{<}{} +: CN^- \longrightarrow \overset{\displaystyle >}{C} - \overset{\cdot\cdot}{\underset{\cdot\cdot}{O}}: ^- \quad (-\,E \text{ effect})}$$
$$\underset{CN}{|}$$

Hyperconjugation

it is the delocalisation of sigma electron. Also known as sigma-pi conjugation or no bond resonance

Occurrence: Alkene, alkynes. Free radicals (saturated type) carbonium ions (saturated type)

Condition: Presence of a–H with respect to double bond, triple bond carbon containing positive charge (in carbonium ion)

Example

$$\underset{\underset{H}{|}}{\overset{\overset{H}{|}}{H-C-CH}} = CH_2 \longleftrightarrow \underset{\underset{H}{|}}{\overset{\overset{H^+}{|}}{H-C-CH}} = \bar{C}H_2 \longleftrightarrow H^+ \underset{\underset{H}{|}}{\overset{\overset{H}{|}}{C-CH}} = \bar{C}H_2 \longleftrightarrow H \underset{\underset{H^+}{|}}{\overset{\overset{H}{|}}{-C-CH}} = \bar{C}H_2$$
$$(I) \qquad\qquad (II) \qquad\qquad (III) \qquad\qquad (IV)$$

Note: Number of hyperconjugative structures = number of a-Hydrogen hence, in above examples structures ii,iii,iv are hyperconjugative structures (H-structures).

Hyperconjugation is a permanent effect

Effects of hyperconjugation

Bond Length: Like resonance, hyperconjugation also affects bond lengths because during the process the single bond in compound acquires some double bond character and vice-versa. E.g. C—C bond length in propene is 1.488 Å as compared to 1.334Å in ethylene .

H—C—CH = CH$_2$ ⟷ H——C =CH—C̄H$_2$

1.353 Å   1.353 Å   1.488Å   1.488 Å   H$^+$

Dipole moment : Since hyperconjugation causes the development of charges, it also affects the dipole moment of the molecule.

Stability of carbonium Ions: The order of stability of carbonium ions is as follows. Tertiary > Secondary > Primary

above order of stability can be explained by hyperconjugation. In general greater the number of hydrogen atoms attached to a-carbon atoms, the more hyperconjugative forms can be written and thus greater will be the stability of carbonium ions.

Stability of Free radicals: Stability of Free radicals can also be explained as that of carbonium ion

$$(CH_3)_3 \overset{\bullet}{C} > (CH_3)_2 \overset{\bullet}{C}H > CH_3 \overset{\bullet}{C}H_2 > \overset{\bullet}{C}H_3$$

CHAPTER 4

REACTIVE INTERMEDIATES

A reactive intermediate or an intermediate as a molecular entity (atom, ion, molecule...) with a life time appreciably longer than a molecular vibration that is formed (directly or indirectly) from the reactants and reacts further to give(either directly or indirectly) the products of a chemical reaction. It is a short-lived, high-energy, highly reactive molecule. When generated in a chemical reaction, it will quickly convert into a more stable molecule.

The main carbon reactive intermediates are:

(i)Carbocations

(ii) Carbanions

(iii) Free radicals and

(iv)Carbenes

(i)Carbocations

Carbocations are carbon atoms in an organic molecule bearing a positive formal charge. Therefore they are carbon cations. Carbocations have only six electrons in their valence shell making them electron deficient. Thus, they are unstable electrophiles and will react very quickly with nucleophiles to form new bonds.

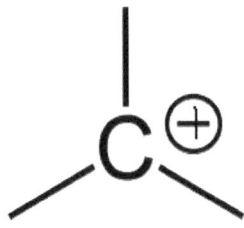

Carbocation Structure

The orbitals of carbocations are generally sp2 hybridized so that the three full orbitals are arranged in a trigonal planar geometry about the carbon nucleus. The remaining p orbital is empty and will readily accept a pair of electrons from another atom. Because of the symmetry of this geometric arrangement, nucleophilic attack is equally favorable above or below the plane formed by the full orbitals.

empty unhybridized
'p' orbital

120^0

$+$

sp^2 hybridized carbon

the p-orbital that is not utilised in the hybrids is empty and is often shown bearing the positive charge since it represents the orbital available to accept electrons.

kinds of carbocations

Primary carbocations

In a primary (1°) carbocation, the carbon which carries the positive charge is only attached to one other alkyl group.

Some examples of primary carbocations include:

$$CH_3 - \overset{+}{C}H_2 \qquad CH_3CH_2 - \overset{+}{C}H_2 \qquad CH_3\underset{\underset{CH_3}{|}}{CH} - \overset{+}{C}H_2$$

Secondary carbocations

In a secondary (2°) carbocation, the carbon with the positive charge is attached to two other alkyl groups, which may be the same or different.

Examples:

$$CH_3 - \overset{+}{C}H - CH_3 \qquad CH_3CH_2 - \overset{+}{C}H - CH_3 \qquad CH_3\underset{\underset{CH_3}{|}}{CH} - \overset{+}{C}H - CH_3$$

Tertiary carbocations

In a tertiary (3°) carbocation, the positive carbon atom is attached to three alkyl groups, which may be any combination of same or different.

$$CH_3 - \overset{+}{\underset{\underset{CH_3}{|}}{C}} - CH_3 \qquad CH_3CH_2 - \overset{+}{\underset{\underset{CH_3}{|}}{C}} - CH_3 \qquad CH_3CH_2 - \overset{+}{\underset{\underset{CH_2CH_2CH_3}{|}}{C}} - CH_3$$

Carbocation Stability

Order of stability of carbocations

primary < secondary < tertiary

Formation of Carbocations

Carbocation intermediates are formed in three main types of reactions: additions to pi bonds, unimolecular eliminations, and unimolecular nucleophilic substitution. On a bridge head a positive carbon is rare. The 3-cyclopropyl carbocation is the most stable carbocation.

Reactions of Carbocations

In general, carbocations will undergo three basic types of reactions:

1. Nucleophile Capture

Carbocations will react with even mild nucleophiles (such as water) to form a new bond.and formation of carbon free radical

2. Elimination to form a pi bond

Carbons alpha to the carbocation will often lose a proton to form a double (or, in some cases) triple bond from the carbocation. Such a reaction requires only a mild base (e.g. chloride) to remove the proton.

3. Rearrangement

A secondary carbocation may rearrange to form a tertiary carbocation before the ion is stabilized using one of the above-mentioned reactions. Since a cation constitutes a deficiency of electrons, the empty orbitals do not move; rather, a hydrogen atom bonded to a nearby carbon is moved to stabilize the secondary carbocation, of the hydrogen atom creates a new tertiary carbocation, which is more stable and will be substituted to lead to the final product.

Factors that stabilize Carbocations

Carbocations are stabilized by neighboring carbon atoms.

The stability of carbocations increases as we go from primary to secondary to tertiary carbons.

1. Increasing substitution by carbon stabilizes carbocations

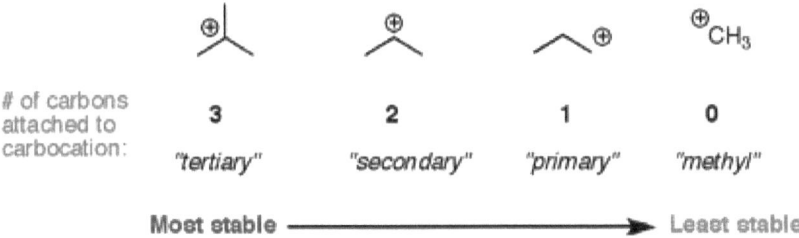

# of carbons attached to carbocation:	3	2	1	0
	"tertiary"	*"secondary"*	*"primary"*	*"methyl"*

Most stable ⟶ Least stable

Carbocations are stabilized by neighboring carbon-carbon multiple bonds. Carbocations adjacent to another carbon-carbon double or triple bond have special stability because overlap between the empty p orbital of the carbocation with the p orbitals of the π bond allows for charge to be shared between multiple atoms. This effect, called "delocalization"

2. Adjacent carbon-carbon π bonds stabilize carbocations

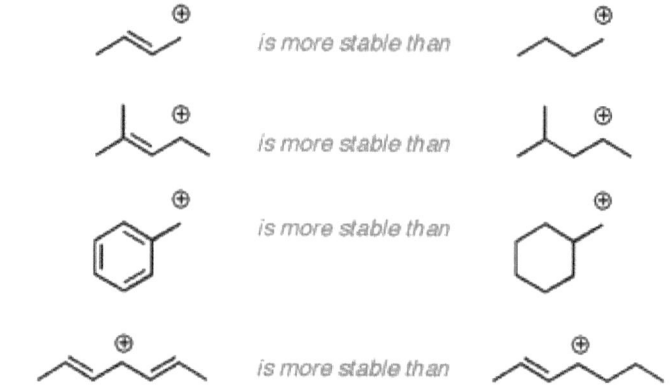

(note how the effect is additive)

Why? Resonance.

Resonance allows for the positive charge to be distributed over multiple carbons, which is a stabilizing influence.

This carbocation cannot be stabilized by resonance.

Carbocations are stabilized by adjacent lone pairs. The key stabilizing influence is a neighboring atom that donates a pair of electrons to the electron-poor carbocation. This results in forming a double bond (π bond) and the charge will move to the atom donating the electron pair. Hence this often goes by the name of "π donation"

3. Adjacent atoms with lone pairs stabilize carbocations

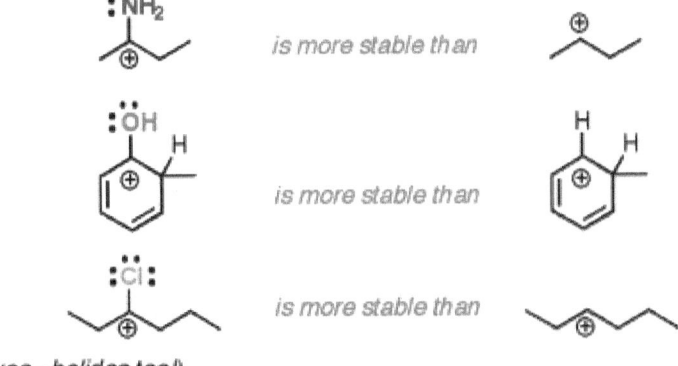

is more stable than

is more stable than

is more stable than

(yes - halides too!)

Why? Resonance (again)

Donation of a lone pair by the atom allows for formation of a new π bond, which is a stabilizing influence

Even though Cl is fairly electronegative the lone pair can still form a π bond!

(ii) Carbanions

Carbanions are units that contain a negative charge on a carbon atom. The negative charge gives good nucleophilic properties to the unit that can be used in the formation of new carbon carbon bonds.

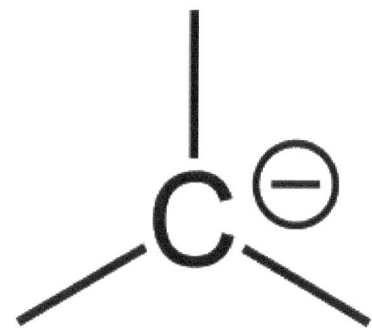

Characteristic of Carbanions :

(i)   Hybridisation and geometry : Alkyl carbanion has three bond pairs and one lone pair. Thus hybridisation is sp3 and geometry is pryamidal.

Note : Geometry of allyl and benzyl cabanion is almost planar and hybridisation is sp2.

(ii)   There are eight electrons in the outermost orbit of carbanionic carbon hence its octet is complete.

(iii) It behaves as charged nucleophile.

(iv) It is diamagnetic in character because all eight electrons are paired.

(v) It is formed by heterolytic bond fission.

(vi) It reacts with electrophiles.

2) Stability of carbonions : The stability of carbanion may be explained by

(A) Electronegativity of carbanionic carbon :

Stability directly propotional to electronegativity of carbaionic carbon which is directly propptional to

% s-character of carbanionic carbon

$$CH3 - \qquad CH2 = \qquad CH°$$

$$sp3 \qquad sp2 \qquad sp$$

(i) % s-character in increasing order

(ii) Stability in increasing order.

(B) Inductive effect : Stability of carbanions depends on the +I or – I group as follows

1. with increase in +I effect stability decreases

2. with increase in –I effect stability increases

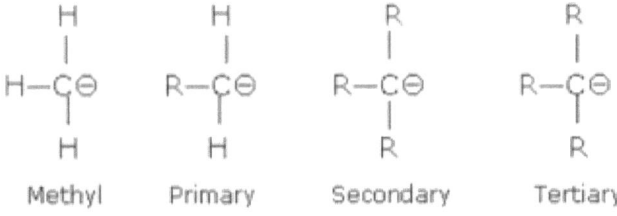

(i)+I in increasing order (ii) Stability in decreasing order.

(C) Delocalistion or Resonance : Allyl and benzyl carbanions are stabilised by delocalisation of negative charge.

$CH_2 = CH - CH_2$- $C_6H_5 - CH_2$- $(C_6H_5)_2 - CH_2$- $(C_6H_5)_3 - CH_2$-

7   10   2   4

    (i) Number of resonating structures in increasing order

    (ii) Stability in increasing order

(D) Stabilisation by Sulphur and Phosphorous: Attachment of carbanionic carbon of a sulphur and phosphorus atom causes an increase in carbanion stability.

The cause of stability is due to the delocalisation of negative charge of carbanion by vaccant d-orbital (p pi–dpi bonding) of phosphorus and sulphur.

(E) Stabilisation by $>C=O$, $-NO_2$ and CN groups present on carbanionic carbon : These groups stabilise carbanion by resonance effect

    Carbanion   Enolate ion

      (I)   (II)

Contribution of structure (II) will be more than (I) because in (II) negative charge is present on electronegative oxygen.

(F) Stability of Aromatic Carbanions :

(i) Anions in which negative charge is present on carbon of aromatic system is known as aromatic carbanions.

(ii) Aromatic carbanions are most stable carbaions.

(iii) Anions obeying Huckel rule are stable because they are aromatic and there is complete delocalisation of negative charge.

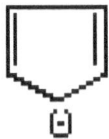

Cyclopentadienyl anion

(3) Stability of different type of carbanions in decreasing order :

　　　Aromatic carbanion > Benzyl carbanion > Allyl carbanion > CH= > CH2 = > Alkyl carbanion

(4) Reactions in which product formation takes place by formation of carbanion as reaction intermediate :

In the following reactions product formation takes place by the formation of carbanion as reaction　intermediates :

(i) Condensation reactions of carbonyl compounds, i.e., aldol condensation, Perkin reaction, reformatsky　reaction, manich reaction, Michael reaction

(ii) Condensation reactions of ester; Claisen condensation.

(iii) Wittig reaction.

Structure

Carbanions are trivalent with sp3hybridization. The lone pare of electrons occupies one of the sp3 orbitals. The geometery is thus tetrahedral. The tetrahedron can undergo inversion or retain its stereochemistry depending on the attached substitutents.

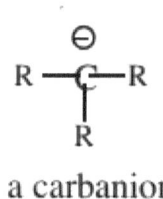

a carbanion

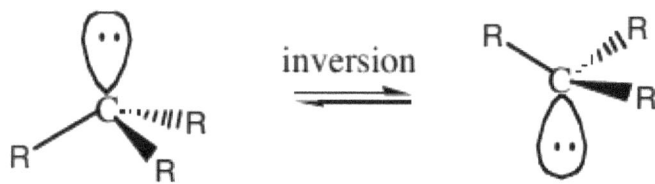

inversion

R = H; barrier = 2 kcal/mole

R = F; barrier = 120 kcal/mole

tetrahedral carbanion

Effect of Substituents on Carbanion Stability

Hybridization

The fractional s-character of the C-H bonds has a major effect on the kinetic and thermodynamic acidity of the carbon acid. Only s-orbitals have electron density at the nucleus, and a lone pair with high fractional s character has its electron density closer to the nucleus, and is hence stabilized. This can be easily seen in the gas-phase acidity of the prototypical C-H types, ethane, ethylene and acetylene, as well as for cyclopropane, where the hybridization of the C-H bond is similar to that in ethylene.

$$CH_3\text{-}CH_3 \qquad \triangle \qquad CH_2\text{=}CH_2 \qquad HC\equiv CH$$

ΔH°_{acid} (kcal/mol)	420	411	406	375

These effects are also clearly evident in solution, with terminal acetylenes and highly strained hydrocarbons easily metalated by strong bases.

2. Inductive Effects

Electron-withdrawing substituents will inductively stabilize negative charge on nearby carbons. These effects are complex, since electronegative substituents interact with carbanions in other ways as well (e.g. O and F substituents have lone pairs, which tend to destabilize adjacent carbanion centers).

pK$_a$ (DMSO)	29.0	31.0	30.7	28.5	19.4

3. Conjugation - π Delocalization

Delocalization of negative charge, especially onto electronegative atoms, provides potent stabilizations of carbanionic centers. Since almost all conjugating substituents are also more electronegative than H or CH3, there is usually a significant inductive contribution to the stabilization.

	CH₄		-CH₃					
pKₐ (DMSO)	~55		43		26.5		30.3	31.3

A special case is the aromatic stabilization of cyclopentadienide and related indenide and fluorenide anions (Hückel 4n + 2 π electron rule) .

pKₐ (DMSO)	18.0	20.1	22.6	30.1

ΔH°ₐcᵢd (kcal/mol)	356.1	373.9

The aromatic anions (6e π system) show a level of stabilization far above that of normal conjugated systems

4. Second and Third Row Element Effects ("d-orbital" effects)

All measures of acidity show that there is an unusual level of carbanion stabilization for all second row elements (Cl, S, P, Si, as well as higher elements) when these are bonded to a carbanion center.

	Me	OMe	OPh	SPh	SePh
pK$_a$ (DMSO)	24.4	22.9	21.1	17.1	18.6

Gas phase acidity

	FCH$_3$	MeOCH$_3$	Me-CH$_3$
ΔH°$_{acid}$ (kcal/mol)	409	407	420.1

	ClCH$_3$	MeSCH$_3$	Me$_3$SiCH$_3$
ΔH°$_{acid}$ (kcal/mol)	395.6	393.2	390.9
ΛΛH°....	13.4	13.8	19.2

The origin of this stabilization has several components. Classical overlap of the lone pair with the empty d-orbitals is only a minor contributor, since the d-orbitals are too diffuse and too high in energy. Thus both the overlap integral and the eneogy separation are unfavorable. For the electronegative elements (Cl and S) there is an inductive component. For SR, PR$_2$, SiR$_3$ and higher analogs, which bear substituents on the X group, there is a major contribution of σ-hyperconjugation (delocalization of charge into X-R σ* orbitals).

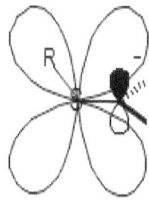
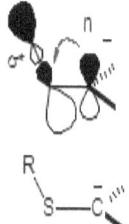

d-orbital interaction   Negative hyperconjugation

A factor comparable in size to σ-hyperconjugation is the σ bond strength effect. There is a size difference between the 3p orbitals of the S and 2p orbitals in the C-H compound. In the carbanion the C orbital increases in size, resulting in a stronger sigma bond. In an oxygen-substituted system the orbital mismatch is in the opposite direction: the p orbital at oxygen is smaller than that at carbon, and this size difference is excacerbated in the carbanion. Superimposed on these effects are possible lone pair effects (Cl, S, P).

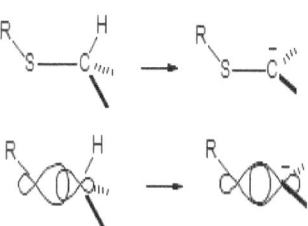

σ bond is stronger in S-substituted carbanions because of better orbital size match (negative charge increases size of C-S orbital)

σ bond is weaker in O-substituted carbanion because of poorer orbital size match

5. Lone Pair Effects

For the first row elements N, O, F, and perhaps also for higher elements, the presence of lone pairs has a strong destabilizing effect on a directly bonded carbanion center. This has several effects on carbanion structure: there are substantial rotational barriers around the C-X bond and the carbanion center is usually more pyramidalized.

Free radicals

Free radicals are atoms or groups of atoms with an odd (unpaired) number of electrons and can be formed when oxygen interacts with certain molecules.

Formation

Free radicals can be generated both in-vivo and in-vitro by one of the following mechanisms:

1. Homolytic cleavage of a covalent bond, in which a normal molecule fragments in two, each fragment retaining one of the paired electrons. Homolytic cleavage occurs less commonly in biological systems, as it requires high-energy input from ultra-violet light, heat or ionising radiation.

2. Loss of a single electron from a normal molecule.

3. Addition of an electron to a normal molecule.

Reactivity

The order of stability of carbon free radicals is:

tertiary > secondary > primary > methyl

Stability of Radicals

Due to the unpaired electrons, free radicals do not have an electron octet. Therefore, they are usually instable and highly reactive. As a result of their high reactivity, radicals merely show a low selectivity. Thus, radicals are a threat to biological cells.

Much like carbocations, radicals usually appear only during intermediate stages. However, in comparison to carbocations, carbon-centered radicals normally exhibit a longer half-life period. The stability of radicals - as in case of carbocations - depends on their structure. Higherly substituted radicals are, in comparison, more stable than lower substituted ones. The stability of radicals can be determined by the dissociation energies of the C-H bonds that must be homolytically cleaved in order to obtain the radicals.

Stabilization by hyperconjugation

The sequence of radical stability may be explained by the differing amounts of hyperconjugation. The more alkyl substituents a radical carbon atom possesses, the more stabilized it becomes from hyperconjugation.

The interaction of the double-occupied C-H σ bonding orbital with the single-occupied, non-bonding p orbital of the radical carbon atom is comparable to the stabilization by hyperconjugation in carbenium ions. However, they differ greatly in one important factor. The stabilization of carbenium ions, for example, is the result of the overlapping of a double-occupied C-H bonding orbital with an unoccupied, non-bonding 2p orbital. In radicals, on the other hand, this stabilization is obtained by the overlapping of a C-H bonding orbital with a single-occupied, non-bonding 2p orbital.

The stability of radicals can also be increased by aromatic substituents at the radical carbon atom. The central radical carbon atom of the triphenylmethyl radical, for instance, carries three phenyl groups. Therefore, the radical is highly resonance-stabilized. The triphenylmethyl radical is, in fact, so stable that it is at equilibrium with a dimer in a solution at room temperature even if the radical consumes only two percent of the equilibrium mixture. However, the large steric hindrance most likely prevents the formation of hexaphenylethane.

Carbenes

a carbene is a molecule containing a neutral carbon atom with a valence of two and two unshared valence electrons. The general formula is R-(C:)-R' or R=C: The term "carbene" may also refer to the specific compound H2C:, also called methylene, the parent hydride from which all other carbene compounds are formally derived.

Carbenes are classified as either singlets or triplets depending upon their electronic structure. Most carbenes are very short lived, although persistent carbenes are known.

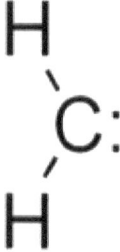

One well studied carbene is dichlorocarbene Cl2C:, which can be generated in situ from chloroform and a strong base.

Structure and bonding

The two classes of carbenes are singlet and triplet carbenes. Singlet carbenes are spin-paired. In the language of valence bond theory, the molecule adopts an sp2 hybrid structure. Triplet carbenes have two unpaired electrons. They may be either linear or bent, i.e. sp or sp2 hybridized, respectively.

singlet   triplet   triplet

Carbenes are called singlet or triplet depending on the electronic spins they possess. Triplet carbenes are paramagnetic and may be observed by electron spin resonance spectroscopy if they persist long enough. The total spin of singlet carbenes is zero while that of triplet carbenes is one (in units of $\hbar$). Bond angles are 125-140° for triplet methylene and 102° for singlet methylene (as determined by EPR). Triplet carbenes are generally stable in the gaseous state, while singlet carbenes occur more often in aqueous media.

For simple hydrocarbons, triplet carbenes usually have energies 8 kcal/mol (33 kJ/mol) lower than singlet carbenes (see also Hund's rule of maximum multiplicity), thus, in general, triplet is the more stable state (the ground state) and singlet is the excited state species. Substituents that can donate electron pairs may stabilize the singlet state by delocalizing the pair into an empty p-orbital. If the energy of the singlet state is sufficiently reduced it will actually become the ground state.

Reactivity

inglet and triplet carbenes exhibit divergent reactivity. Singlet carbenes generally participate in cheletropic reactions as either electrophiles or nucleophiles. Singlet carbenes with unfilled p-orbital should be electrophilic. Triplet carbenes can be considered to be diradicals, and participate in stepwise radical additions. Triplet carbenes have to go through an intermediate with two unpaired electrons whereas singlet carbene can react in a single concerted step.

Due to these two modes of reactivity, reactions of singlet methylene are stereospecific whereas those of triplet methylene are stereoselective. This difference can be used to probe the nature of a carbene. For example, the reaction of methylene generated from photolysis of diazomethane with cis-2-butene or with trans-2-butene each give a single diastereomer of the 1,2-dimethylcyclopropane product: cis from cis and trans from trans, which proves that the methylene is a singlet. If the methylene were a triplet, one would not expect the product to depend upon the starting alkene geometry, but rather a nearly identical mixture in each case.

Reactivity of a particular carbene depends on the substituent groups. Their reactivity can be affected by metals. Some of the reactions carbenes can do are insertions into C-H bonds, skeletal rearrangements, and additions to double bonds. Carbenes can be classified as nucleophilic, electrophilic, or ambiphilic. For example, if a substituent is able to donate a pair of electrons, most likely carbene will not be electrophilic. Alkyl carbenes insert much more selectively than methylene, which does not differentiate between primary, secondary, and tertiary C-H bonds.

Cyclopropanation

Carbenes add to double bonds to form cyclopropanes. A concerted mechanism is available for singlet carbenes. Triplet carbenes do not retain stereochemistry in the product molecule. Addition reactions are commonly very fast and exothermic. The slow step in most instances is generation of carbene. A well-known reagent employed for alkene-to-cyclopropane reactions is Simmons-Smith reagent. This reagent is a system of copper, zinc, and iodine, where the active reagent is believed to be iodomethylzinc iodide.

The Simmons–Smith reaction is an organic cheletropic reaction involving an organozinc carbenoid that reacts with an alkene (or alkyne) to form a cyclopropane

$$Zn/Cu + CH_2I_2 \longrightarrow IZnCH_2I$$

Bicyclo[4.1.0]heptane

Bamford-Stevens reaction

The Bamford-Stevens reaction is a chemical reaction which can convert a ketone into an alkene via treatment with a tosylhydrazone and a strong base. The reaction forms a diazo compound as an intermediate which may be isolated.

Step 1

Step 2

C—H insertion

Insertions are another common type of carbene reactions. The carbene basically interposes itself into an existing bond. The order of preference is commonly: 1. X–H bonds where X is not carbon 2. C–H bond 3. C–C bond. Insertions may or may not occur in single step.

Intramolecular insertion reactions present new synthetic solutions. Generally, rigid structures favor such insertions to happen. When an intramolecular insertion is possible, no intermolecular insertions are seen. In flexible structures, five-membered ring formation is preferred to six-membered ring formation. Both inter- and intramolecular insertions are amendable to asymmetric induction by choosing chiral ligands on metal centers.

Transition Metal Carbene Complexes

The transition metal carbene complexes can be classified according to their reactivity, with the first two classes being the most clearly defined:

Fischer carbenes, in which the carbene is bonded to a metal that bears an electron-withdrawing group (usually a carbonyl). In such cases the carbenoid carbon is mildly electrophilic.

Schrock carbenes, in which the carbene is bonded to a metal that bears an electron-donating group. In such cases the carbenoid carbon is nucleophilic and resembles Wittig reagent (which are not considered carbene derivatives).

Persistent carbenes, also known as Arduengo or Wanzlick carbenes. These include the class of N-heterocyclic carbenes (NHCs) and are often are used as ancillary ligands in organometallic chemistry. Such carbenes are spectator ligands of low reactivity.

CHAPTER 5

TYPES OF ORGANIC REACTIONS

Types of Organic Reactions

All organic reactions can be broadly classified into four catagories.

1. **Elimination reactions**
2. **Substitution reactions**
3. **Addition reactions and**
4. **Rearrangement reactions**

1.Elimination Reactions

An elimination reaction is one which involves the loss of two atoms or groups of atoms from the same or adjacent atoms of a substrate molecule leading to formation of multiple (double or triple) bond. These are of two types.

β - elimination reactions: In these reactions, loss of two atoms or groups occurs from the adjacent atoms of the substrate molecule. This reaction is also known as 1,2- or α,β- elimination or β - elimination.

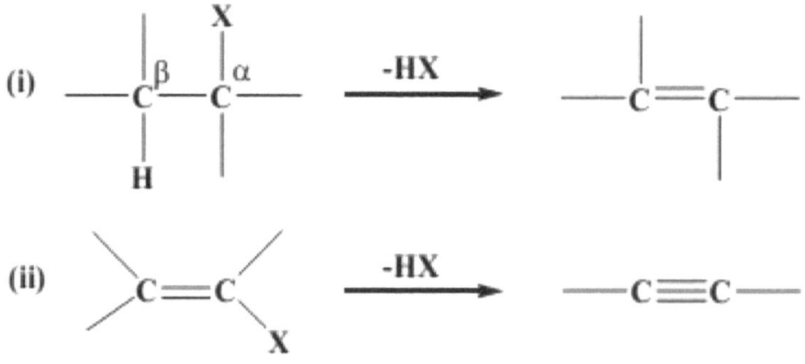

Some similar elimination reactions are

(1) Dehydrohalogenation of alkyl halide by base.

$$RCH_2CH_2-X \xrightarrow{\overset{\ominus}{OH}} RCH=CH_2 \quad H_2O + \overset{\ominus}{X}$$

(2) Dehydration of alcohols by acids

$$RCH_2CH_2-OH \xrightarrow{\overset{\oplus}{H}} RCH=CH_2 \quad + H_2O + \overset{\oplus}{H}$$

(3) Hofmann's degradation of quaternary bases by heat.

$$RCH_2CH_2-\overset{\oplus}{N}R_3\overset{\ominus}{OH} \xrightarrow{\Delta} RCH=CH_2 \quad + R_3N + H_2O$$

The presence of at least one hydrogen atom on the b carbon is necessary for elimination.

The driving forces for elimination are

(a) Stability of the olefin formed

(b) The relief from steric strain due to crowding in the substrate.

Branching at the b carbon of the substrate produces substituted olefins stabilized by hyperconjugation and hence favors elimination.Strain in the substrate due to crowding by the substituents can be relieved on the formation of olefin since the

The elimination reaction may proceed by either unimolecular E_1 or bimolecular E_2 mechanism.

E_1 mechanism

The E1 mechanism is a two step process in which the rate determining step is ionization of the substrate to give a carbocation that rapidly loses a β - proton to a base.

Step 1

$$-\overset{\displaystyle |}{\underset{\displaystyle H}{C}}-\overset{\displaystyle |}{\underset{\displaystyle |}{C}}-X \underset{}{\overset{\text{Slow}}{\rightleftharpoons}} H-\overset{\displaystyle |}{\underset{\displaystyle |}{C}}-\overset{\displaystyle |}{\underset{\displaystyle |}{C}}{}^{\oplus} + X^{\ominus}$$

Step 2

$$-\overset{\displaystyle |}{\underset{\displaystyle H}{C}}-\overset{\displaystyle |}{\underset{\displaystyle |}{C}}{}^{\oplus} \overset{\text{Solvent}}{\longrightarrow} -\overset{\displaystyle |}{C}=\overset{\displaystyle |}{C}-$$

$$-\overset{H}{\underset{|}{C}}-\overset{|}{\underset{X}{C}}- \overset{\text{slow}}{\longrightarrow} -\overset{H}{\underset{|}{C}}-\overset{|}{C}{}^{+}- + X^{-}$$

$$B: \quad -\overset{H}{\underset{|}{C}}-\overset{|}{C}{}^{+}- \overset{\text{fast}}{\longrightarrow} \;>C=C< + H:B$$

E_1 mechanism reaction the product should be completely nonstereospecific, since the carbocation is free to adopt its most stable conformation.

E₁ Mechanism For Alcohols

H-C-C-OH $\xrightarrow{\overset{+}{H}}$ C=C   H-OH

Step1:

An acid/base reaction. Protonation of the alcoholic oxygen to make a better leaving group. This step is very fast and reversible. The lone pairs on the oxygen make it a Lewis base.

Step2:

Cleavage of the C-O bond allows the loss of the good leaving group, a neutral water molecule, to give a carbocation intermediate. This is the rate determining step (bond breaking is endothermic)

Step3:

An acid/base reaction. Deprotonation by a base (a water molecule) from a C atom adjacent to the carbocation center leads to the creation of the C=C

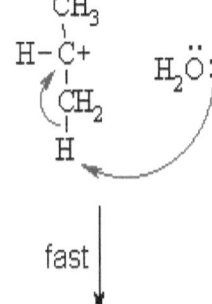

E_1 **Mechanism For Alkyl Halides**

$$\begin{array}{c} H_3C \\ | \\ H-C-Br: \\ | \\ H_3C \end{array}$$

$$\begin{array}{cc} H-\overset{|}{\underset{|}{C}}-\overset{|}{\underset{|}{C}}-X & \xrightarrow{\overset{B^-}{\quad}} \quad \overset{\backslash}{\underset{/}{C}}=\overset{/}{\underset{\backslash}{C}} \quad H-X \end{array}$$

$X = I, Br, Cl, (F)$

slow

$$\begin{array}{c} CH_3 \\ | \\ H-C+ \qquad R\overset{..}{\underset{..}{O}}:^- \\ | \\ CH_2 \\ | \\ H \end{array}$$

Step1:

Cleavage of the polarised C-X bond allows the loss of the good leaving group, a halide ion, to give a carbocation intermediate. This is the rate determining step (bond breaking is endothermic)

fast

$$\begin{array}{c} H \qquad CH_3 \\ \diagdown C \diagup \\ \| \\ \diagup C \diagdown \\ H \qquad H \end{array}$$

$R\overset{..}{\underset{..}{O}}H$

Step2:

An acid/base reaction. Deprotonation by a base (here an alkoxide ion) from a C atom adjacent to the carbocation center leads to the creation of the C=C

Evidence for E_1 mechanism

1. The reaction exhibits first order kinetics as expected. Solvent does not appear in the rate equation, even if it were involved in the rate determining step, but this point can be checked by adding a small amount of the conjugate base of the solvent. This addition does not increase the rate of the reaction. An example of an E1 mechanism with a rate determining second step has been reported.

2. If the reaction is performed on two molecules that differ in the leaving group the rates should obviously be different. Since, they depend on the ionizing ability of the molecule.

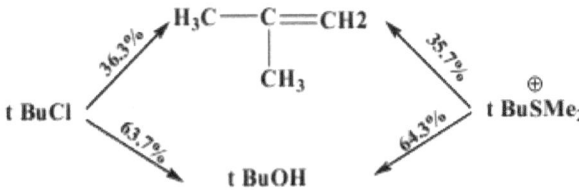

3. If carbocations are intermediates, we expect rearrangements with suitable substrates. These have often been found in elimination reaction performed under E conditions. E1 reactions can involve ion pair. This effect is naturally greatest for nondissociating solvents.

E_1 reaction is facilitated by:

- Branching at the a and b carbons of the substrate –for the stability of the olefin.

- Strongpolar solvent –to acid ionization.

- Low concentration of base– the greater stability of the alkene over the carbocation makes the extraction of proton easy

E₂ Mechanism

When the rate of elimination reaction is dependent on both the substrate and the reagent the reaction is kinetically second order or bimolecular

Transition state

The base abstracts a proton from the β - carbon; simultaneous departure of the nucleophile takes place from the α - carbon. In the transition state the β- C- H and α-C- X bonds are stretched on the attack of the reagent with incipient π- bond formation

The energy of the transition state will be least when two leaving groups, the αand βcarbons and the attacking base are coplanar in the transition state. Also, the two leaving groups (H and X) should be trans to each other to effect π bond. The two leaving groups

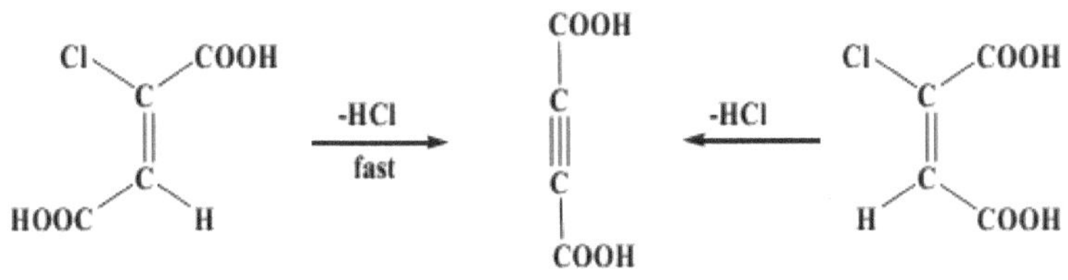

Leaving groups
trans (1)

Leaving groups
cis (2)

Evidences for the existence of E_2 Mechanism

1. The reaction displays the proper second- order kinetics.

2. When the leaving hydrogen is replaced by deuterium in second order elimination there is an isotope effect with breaking of cis bond in the rate determining step. This result proves that E_2 mechanism. E_2 is stereospecific it is found from stereochemical studies.

E_2 reaction is facilitated by:

1. branching at a andb carbons since more stable olefins is formed.

2. Strong base of high concentration since a strong C- H bond has to break.

3. Solvent of lowpolarity

Comparing the E1 and E2 mechanisms		
	E1	E2
Rate Law	Unimolecular (depends on concentration of substrate)	Bimolecular (depends on concentration of both substrate and base)
"Big Barrier"	Formation of carbocation $3° > 2° \gg 1°$	None
Requires strong base?	No	Yes
Stereochemistry	No requirement	Leaving group must be *anti* to hydrogen removed

Exercises

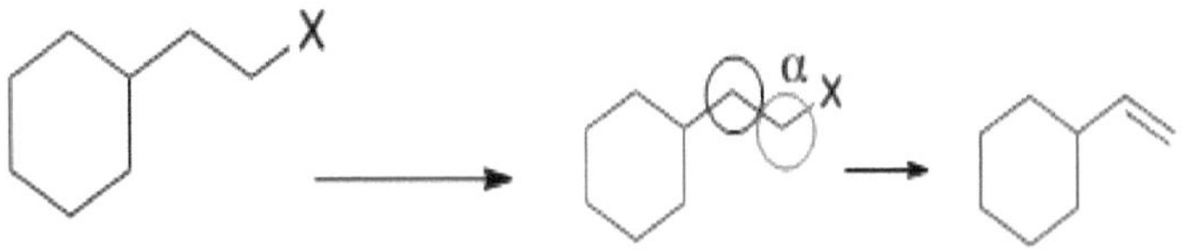
X
α
X

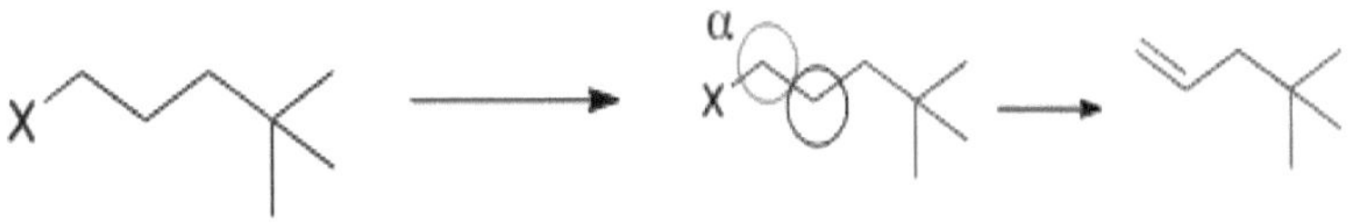
X
α
X

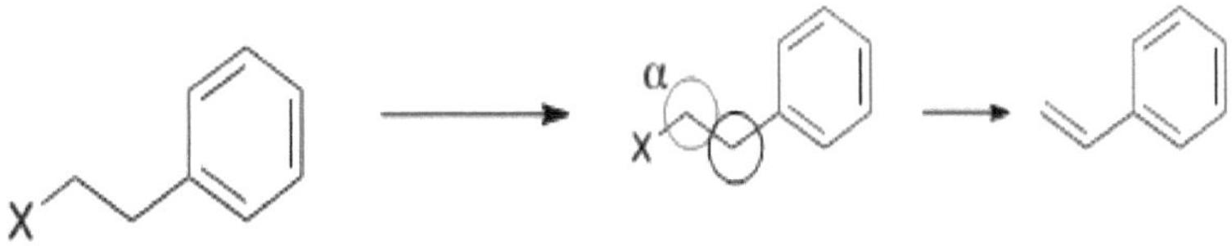
X
α
X

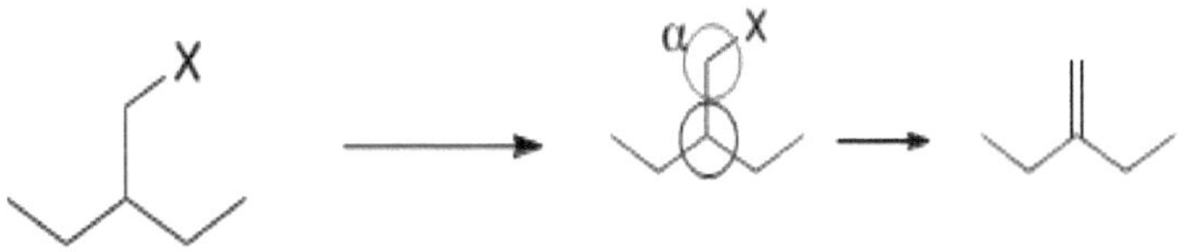
X
α
X

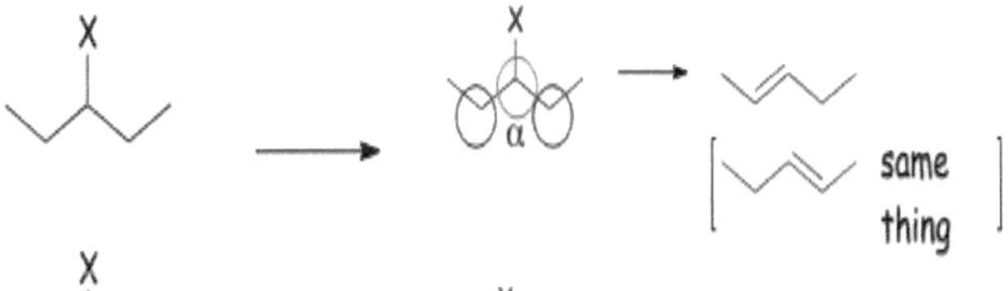
X
X
α
same
thing

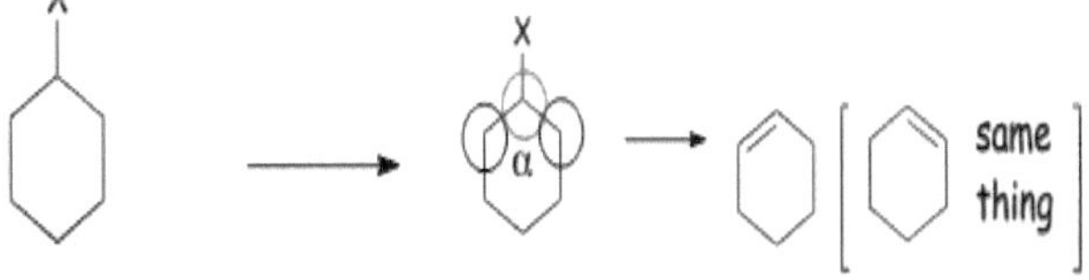
X
X
α
same
thing

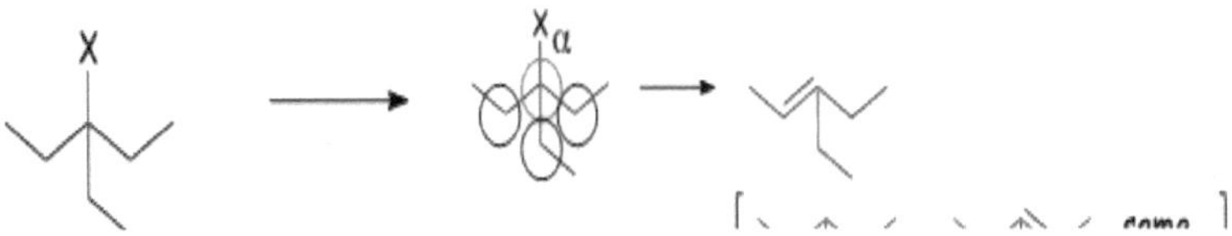
X
X
α

The rate of the E1 reaction depends only on the substrate, since the rate limiting step is the formation of a carbocation. Hence, the more stable that carbocation is, the faster the reaction will be. Forming the carbocation is the "slow step"; a strong base is not required to form the alkene, since there is no leaving group that will need to be displaced (more on that in a second). Finally there is no requirement for the stereochemistry of the starting material; the hydrogen can be at any orientation to the leaving group in the starting material [although we'll see in a sec that we do require that the C-H bond be able to rotate so that it's in the same plane as the empty p orbital on the carbocation when the new π bond is formed.

The rate of the E_2 reaction depends on both substrate and base, since the rate-determining step is bimolecular (concerted). A strong base is generally required, one that will allow for displacement of a polar leaving group. The stereochemistry of the hydrogen to be removed must be *anti* to that of the leaving group; the pair of electrons from the breaking C-H bond donate into the antibonding orbital of the C-(leaving group) bond, leading to its loss as a leaving group.

E_1- CB Mechanism

The second- order elimination reaction may as well proceed in two steps as on E_1 reaction. The first step involved a fast and reversible removal of a proton from the β - carbon with the formation of a carbon ion which then loses the leaving grouping in the second slow rate determining step

$$-\overset{H}{\underset{|}{C}}-\overset{|}{\underset{Br}{C}}- \;+\; EtO^{\ominus} \;\overset{Fast}{\rightleftharpoons}\; -\overset{\ominus}{\underset{|}{C}}-\overset{|}{\underset{Br}{C}}- \;+\; EtOH \quad \cdots\cdots \quad (1)$$

$$-\overset{\ominus}{\underset{|}{C}}-\overset{|}{\underset{Br}{C}}- \;\overset{Slow}{\longrightarrow}\; -\overset{|}{C}{=}\overset{|}{C}- \;+\; Br^{\ominus}$$

The overall rate of this reaction is thus dependent on the concentration of the conjugate base of the substrate. Hence this designated as E_1-CB.

INTRAMOLECULAR ELIMINATION (Ei)

Concerted 1,2- elimination the base is actually part of the substrate molecule. Such elimination can be described as intramolecular. The two groups leave at about the same time and bond to each other as they are doing so. The elimination must be syn, for the four and five membered transition states, the four or five atoms making up the ring must be coplanar.

Evidence for the existence of the E_i mechanism

1. The kinetics is first order, so that only one molecule of the substrate is involved in the reaction.

2. Free - radical inhibitors do not show the reaction. So that, no free - radical mechanism is involved.

3. The mechanism predicts exclusive syn elimination, and this behavior has been found in many cases. The evidence is inverse to that for the anti E2mechanism.

4. ^{14}C isotope effects for the cope elimination show that both the C- H and C - N bonds have been exclusively broken in the transition state.

5. Some of these reactions have been shown to exhibit negative entropies of activation, indicating that the molecules are more restricted on geometry in the transition state

Examples for Ei Mechanism

Acetate esters bearing b , hydrogen's often eliminate acetic acid when pyrolyzed giving the corresponding alkenes. This reaction is found to

(ii) α - Elimination: In these reactions loss of two atoms or groups occurs from the same atom of the substrate molecule. E.g., base catalysed dehydrohalogenation of chloroform to form dichlorocarbene.

Dichlorocarbene is the reactive intermediate involved in carbylamine reaction and Reimer – Tieman reaction.

Stereochemistry of elimination reactions

Eliminations results in p bond formation. In E2 reaction the p-orbital which develops on theα and β carbons with the departure of the leaving group should be parallel for maximum overlap, for this both the leaving groups and carbons bearing them should be in one plane.

When the two leaving groups are planar there are two extreme conformations. Antiperiplanar (i.e.) two groups intransposition, syn- periplanar (i.e.) two groups in cis position. The elimination then may proceed as given below:

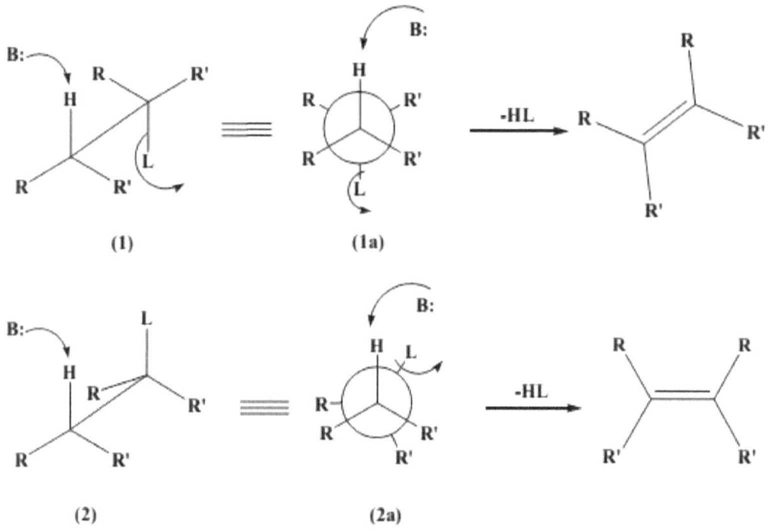

(1)   (1a)

(2)   (2a)

From the Newman projection of the transand cisconformations the elimination is expected to be more facile from the trans conformation 1(a) than from the cis conformation 2(a). This is because in 1(a) the attacking base approaches from the farthest side o the leaving group, while in 2(a) the attack isfrom the same side which causes repulsion. The developing charge on the β - carbon displaces the leaving group with its bonding pair from the backside a path of least energy. The elimination occurs from the lower energy staggered conformation than from the high energy eclipsed conformation

2. SUBSTITUTION REACTIONS

In these an atom or a group of atoms in an organic molecule is replaced by another atom or group of atoms without any change in the remaining part of the molecule. These reactions may be initiated by free radical, electrophile or nucleophile.

(i) Free radical substitution reaction:

This substitution reaction is brought about by free radicals. For example chlorination of methane in presence of diffused sunlight. The mechanism of the reaction is as follows.

$Cl : Cl \rightarrow 2Cl \cdot$ **Chain initiation**

$$CH_4 + Cl^\bullet \rightarrow CH_3^\bullet + HCl$$
$$CH_3^\bullet + Cl_2 \rightarrow CH_3Cl + Cl^\bullet$$
$$CH_3Cl + Cl^\bullet \rightarrow \overset{\bullet}{C}H_2Cl + HCl \left.\right\} \text{Chain propagation}$$

$$Cl^\bullet + Cl^\bullet \rightarrow Cl_2$$
$$\overset{\bullet}{C}H_3 + \overset{\bullet}{C}H_3 \rightarrow CH_3CH_3 \left.\right\} \text{Chain termination}$$

(ii) Nucleophilic substitution reactions:

These reactions are brought about by nucleophile. The reaction can proceed either via SN_1 or SN_2 mechanism.

SN_1 mechanism:

Rate determining step involves only the species. For example the reaction.

$$CH_3-\underset{\underset{CH_3}{|}}{\overset{\overset{CH_3}{|}}{C}}-Br + OH^- \longrightarrow CH_3-\underset{\underset{CH_3}{|}}{\overset{\overset{CH_3}{|}}{C}}-OH + Br^-$$

takes place as follows

1st step: $(CH3)3CBr \xrightarrow[\text{determining step}]{\text{Rate}} (CH_3)C^- + Br^-$ Carbocation

2nd step: Attack by nucleophile

$$(CH_3)_3C^+ + OH^- \longrightarrow CH_3-\underset{\underset{CH_3}{|}}{\overset{\overset{CH_3}{|}}{C}}-OH$$

The stability of carbocation is the controlling factor for this mechanism the formation of $3°$ carbocation as an intermediate proceeds via this mechanism. In an optically active compound substitution at chiral centre through SN_1 mechanism produces recemic mixture (No 100% recemization is observed).

SN$_2$ mechanism: Rate determining step involves two species and reaction proceeds through transition state.

$$CH_3Cl + OH^- \rightarrow CH_3OH + Cl^-$$

Transition state

Since 1° carbocation is less stable than the transition state formed above, the reaction involving 1° alkyl halides proceed via SN2 mechanism. During reaction configuration of carbon is inverted which is referred to as Walden inversion.

Points to Remember

The higher the polarity of solvent greater the tendency for SN_1 reaction.

High concentration of the nucleophile favours SN_2 reaction while low concentration favours SN_1 reaction.

Rearrangement of the carbocation (formed in SN_1 reaction) leading to more stable carbocation is observed in SN_1 reaction (discussed latter).

In general SN_2 mechanism is strongly inhibited by increasing steric bulk of the reagents. In such case SN_1 mechanism is favoured.

Stereochemistry of SN₁ reaction

Since a carbocation is flat (sp², trigonal planar) with the vacant 2p orbital vertical to the plane bearing the three groups, the attack to the reagent can occur from either side of the plane with equal probability, i.e. a racemic product should result if the alkyl halide is chiral

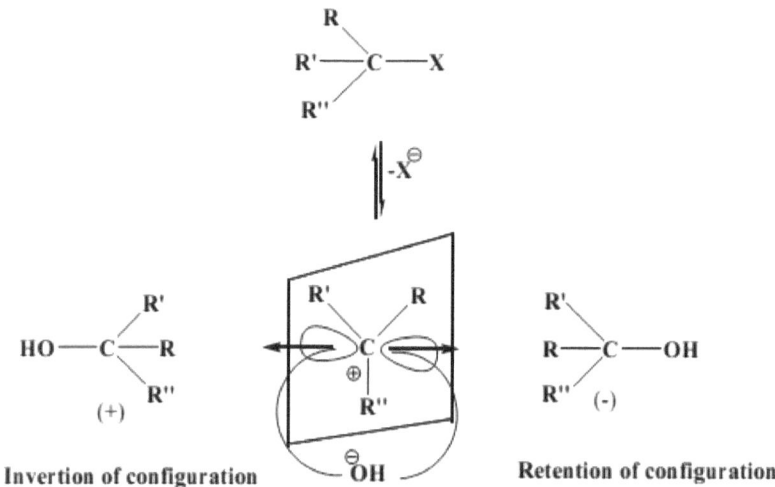

Pure racemisation (50/50 mixture) is rarely observed. This is because the leaving group lies close to the carbocation shielding the side from the attack till it has sufficiently moved away. Thus, more attack of the reagent occurs from the opposite side to the leaving group. This causes more inversion than retention of configuration. Stable carbocations have longer life to permit salvation from either side of the plane of the carbocation resulting in greater proportion of racemisation. Greater proportion of inversion is observed with

Stereochemistry of SN$_2$ reaction

From the course of the direct displacement reaction asshown above, it is seen that the molecule is turned inside out. A Walden inversion is therefore expected to take place. An optically active halide on hydrolysis by SN$_2$ path, therefore, should give an alcohol with inversion of configuration. The change of configuration can be established by observing the directions of optical rotation. In this case, however the substrate (bromide) and the product (alcohol) are two different compounds. The directions of rotation and the configurations of two different compounds are not usually related. Hence, the configurations of the substrate and the product should be related to arrive at the conclusion.

An elegant method has been suggested (Huges and Ingold) to establish the inversion of configuration in SN2 reaction. Themethod involves the conversion of (+2) iodooctane with potassium radioiodide (K ^{128}I) in acetone to (-) 2 - iodooctane. The reaction was found to be bimolecular (SN$_2$).

i.e. rate $\propto [C_6H_{13}CHICH_3] [I^*]$

The exchange of ordinary iodide with the radioactive iodide was accompanied by the loss of optical activity. This indicates the formation of (-) isomer from the (+) isomer to result in racemisation.

The rate of loss of optical activity (i.e. racemisation) was found to be twice the rate of iodine exchange (i.e. inversion) - one (+) molecule is inverted and another (+) molecule pairs with it to form a (±) modification. The above formulated mechanism of SN_2 reaction is therefore established. Inversion of configuration is always indicativeof SN_2 reaction.

Comparing the SN_1 and SN_2 Reactions

	SN_1	SN_2
Rate Law	Unimolecular (Substrate)	Bilmolecular (Substrate and Nucleophile)
Big Barrier	Carbocation stability	Steric hindrance
Alkyl halide (Electrophile)	$3° >2° >>1°$	$1° >2° >>3°$
Nucleophile	Weak	Strong
Solvent	Polar protic e.g alcohol	Polcar aprotic e.g. DMSO, acetone
Stereochemistry	Mix of retention and invesrion	inversion

Exercises on SN_2 Mechanism

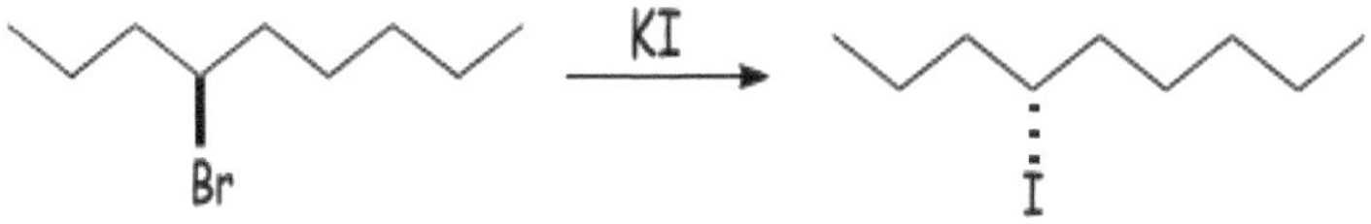
KI
Br
I

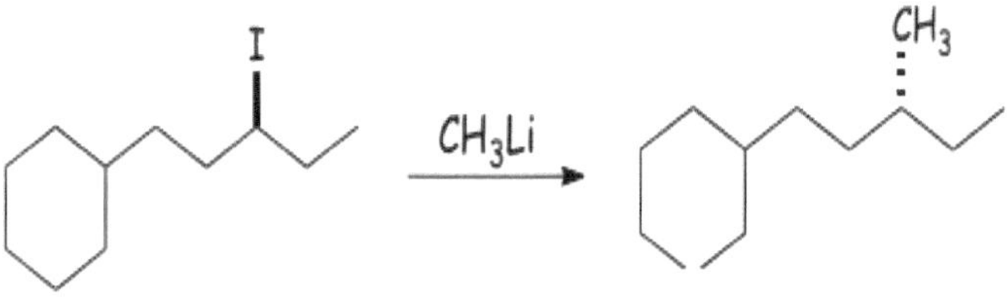
I
CH3Li
CH3

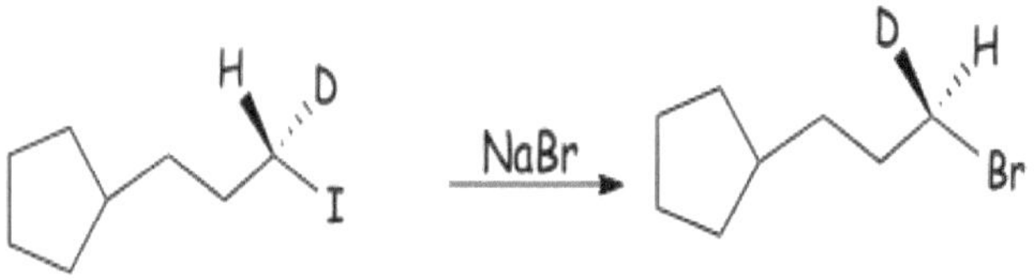
H
D
I
NaBr
D
H
Br

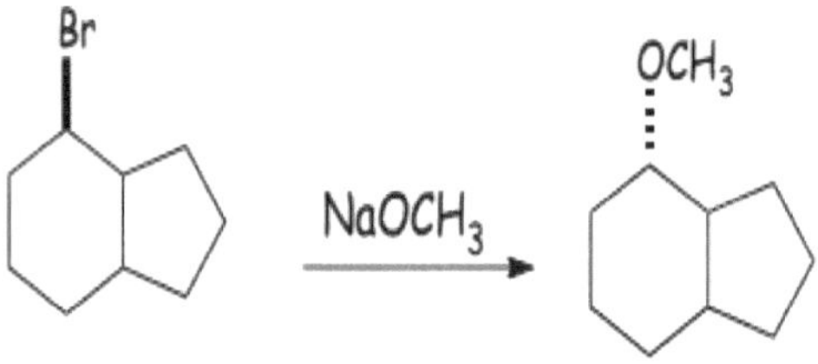
Br
NaOCH3
OCH3

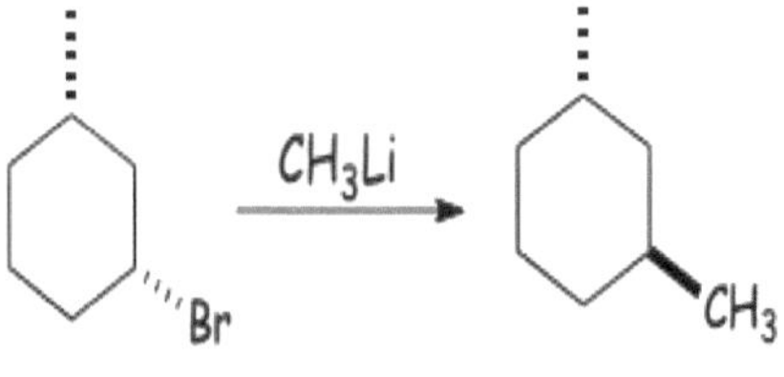
CH3Li
Br
CH3

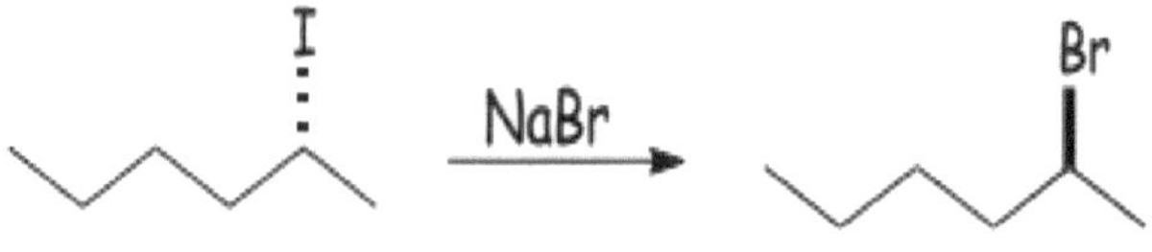
I
NaBr
Br

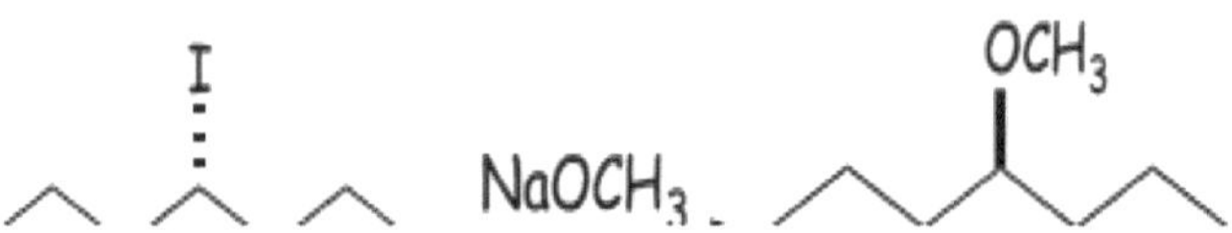
I
NaOCH3
OCH3

SN$_2$

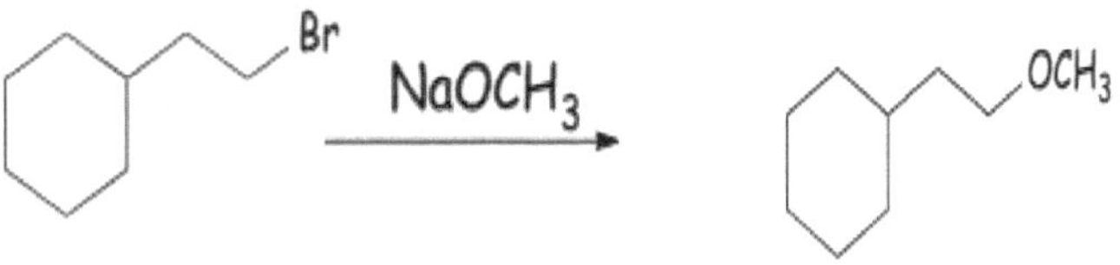

SN$_2$

SN$_1$

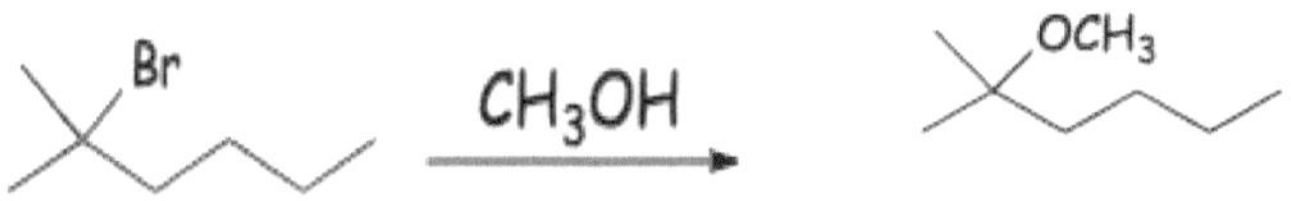

SN$_1$

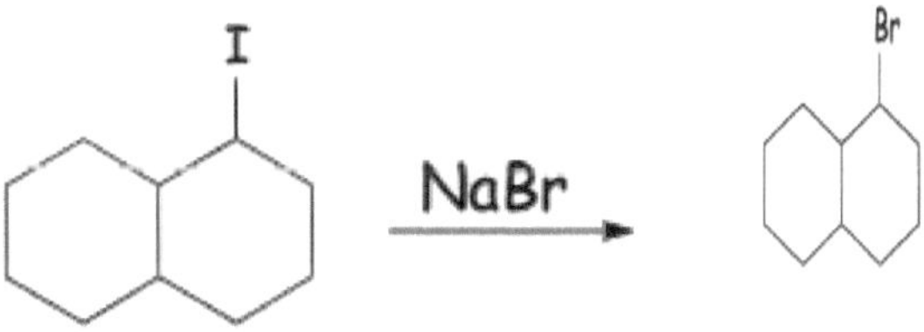

SN$_2$

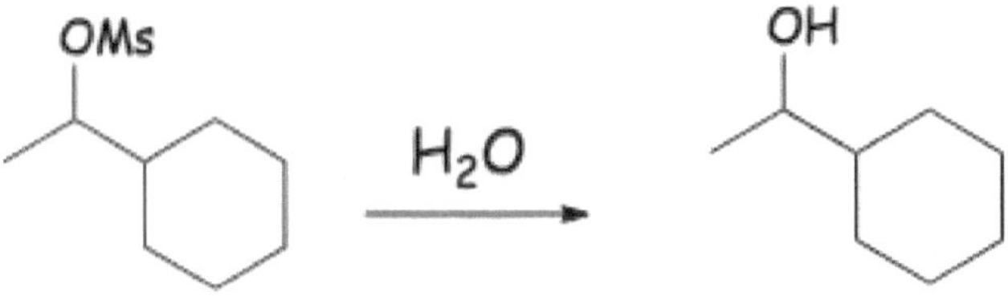

SN$_1$

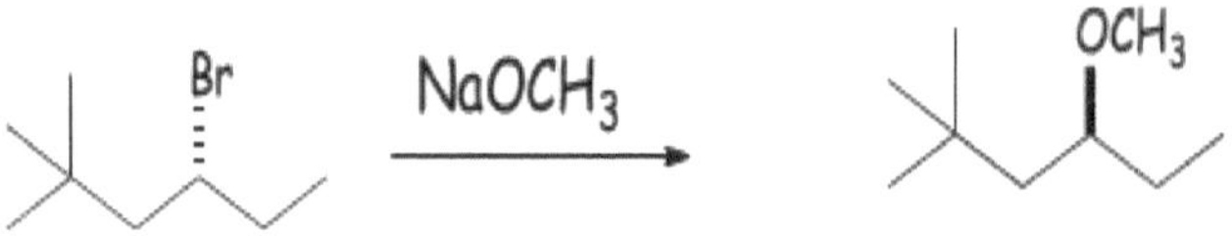

SN$_2$

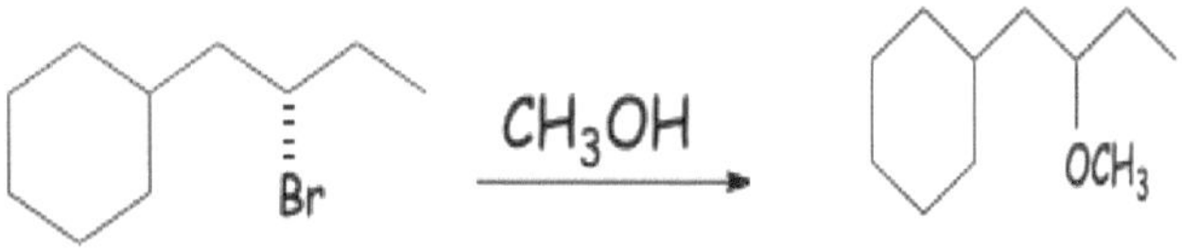

SN$_1$

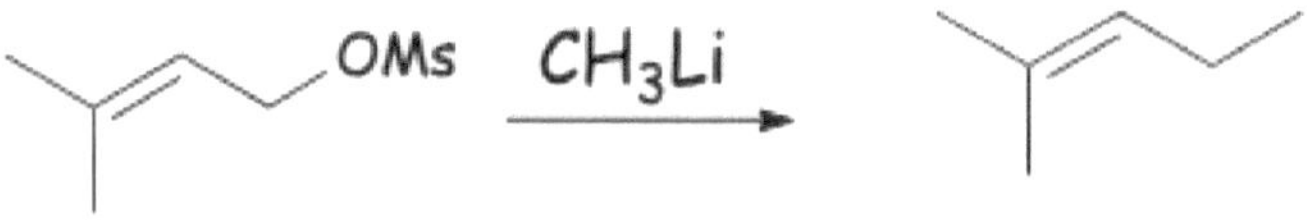

SN$_2$

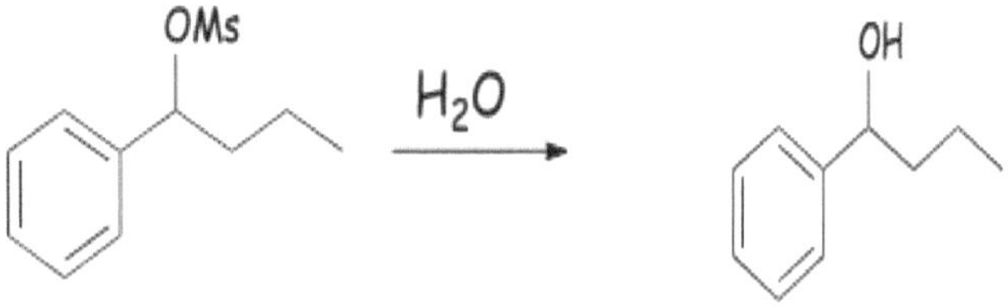

SN$_1$

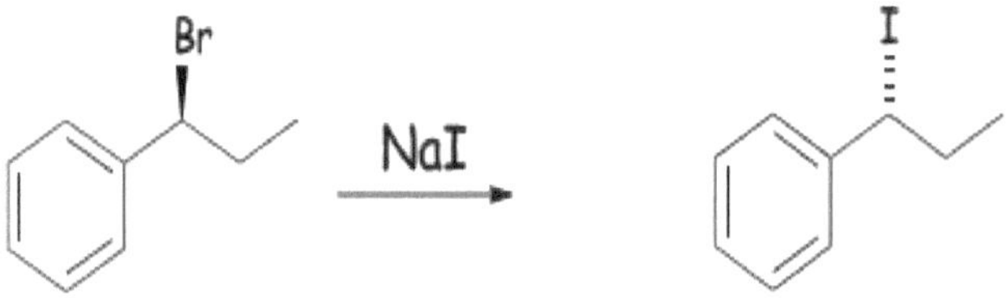

SN$_2$

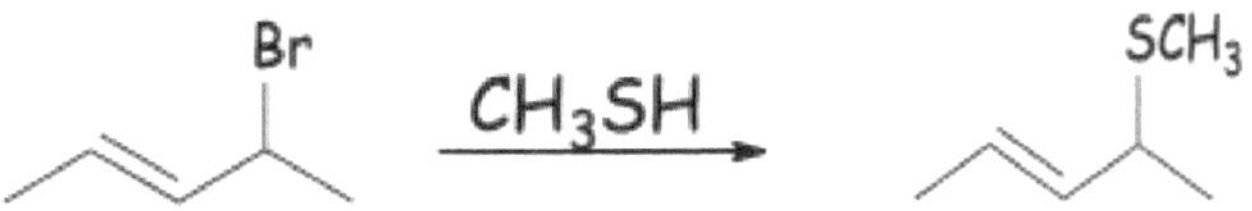

SN$_1$

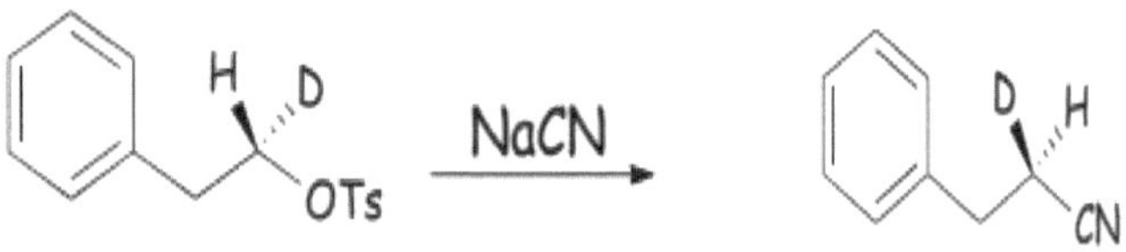

SN$_2$

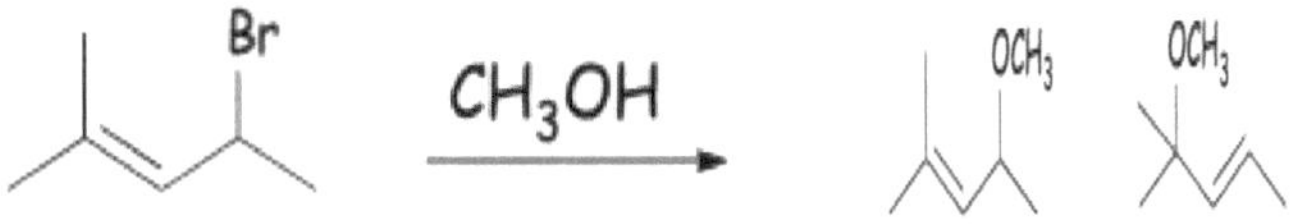

SN$_1$

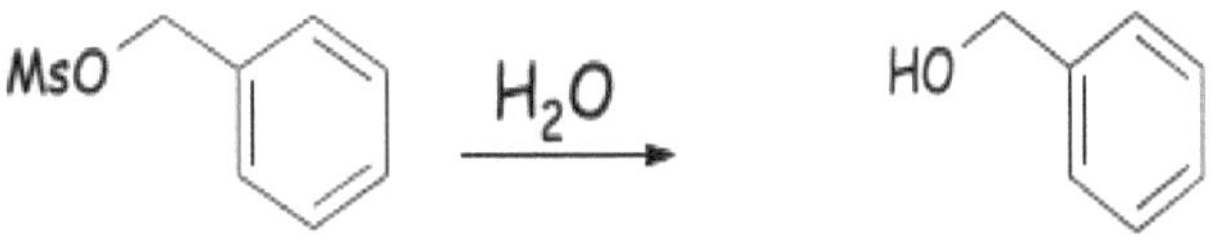

SN$_1$

ii) Electrophilic substitution reactions:

The reaction initiated by an electrophile is known as electrophilic substitution reaction. Aromatic substitution reactions are the examples of this type of reaction.

$$C_6H_6 + Cl_2 \xrightarrow[\text{or AlCl}_3]{\text{FeCl}_3} C_6H_5Cl + HCl$$

The mechanism of this reaction as follows.

Formation of electrophile: $Cl : Cl + AlCl_3 \rightarrow Cl^+ + AlCl_4^-$

Electrophile attack:

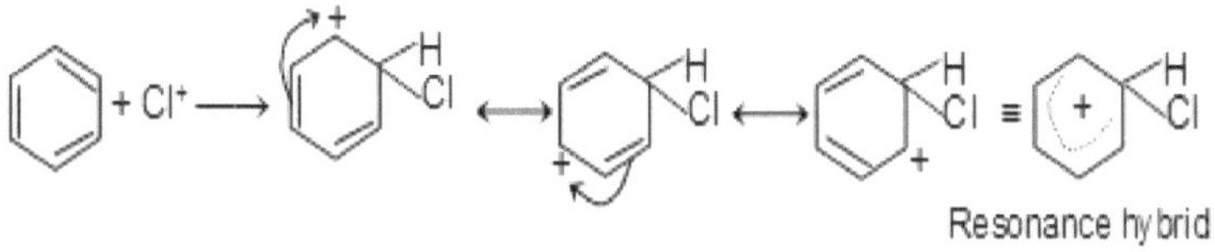

Resonance hybrid

Elimination of proton:

ADDITION REACTIONS

Reactions which involve combination between two molecules to give a single molecule of the product are called addition reactions. Such reactions are typical of compounds containing multiple (double or tripe) bonds.

Depending upon the nature of the attacking species (electrophiles, nucleophiles or free radicals) addition reactions are of the following types.

(i) Electrophilic addition reaction:

These reactions are brought about by electrophiles and are typical reactions of alkenes and alkynes.

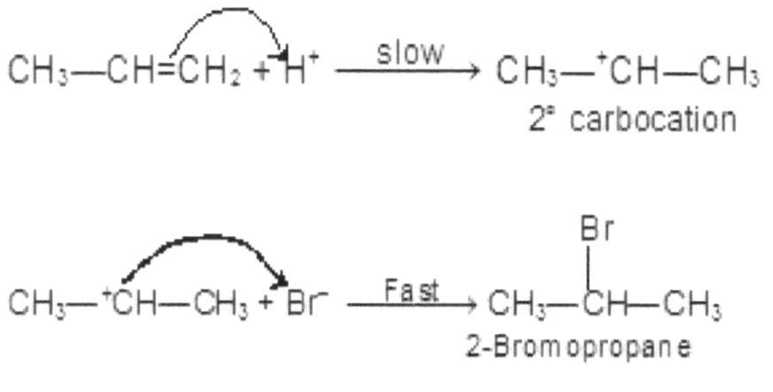

$$CH_3—CH{=}CH_2 + H^+ \xrightarrow{\text{slow}} CH_3—{}^+CH—CH_3$$
$$2^\circ \text{ carbocation}$$

$$CH_3—{}^+CH—CH_3 + Br^- \xrightarrow{\text{Fast}} CH_3—\overset{\displaystyle Br}{\underset{|}{C}}H—CH_3$$
$$\text{2-Bromopropane}$$

Let us take in general the addition of an acidic reagent, HZ, to an alkene

$$\diagdown C = C \diagup + \text{H:Z} \longrightarrow \diagdown \underset{H}{\overset{|}{C}} - \underset{Z}{\overset{|}{C}} \diagup \qquad \text{[HZ = HCl, HBr, HI, H}_2\text{SO}_4\text{]}$$

MECHANISM

(1)

$$\diagdown C = C \diagup + \text{H:Z} \longrightarrow \diagdown \underset{H}{\overset{|}{C}} = \overset{+}{C} \diagup + \text{:Z}$$

(2)

$$\diagdown \underset{H}{\overset{|}{C}} = \overset{+}{\underset{\bullet}{C}} \diagup + \text{:Z} \longrightarrow \diagdown \underset{H}{\overset{|}{C}} - \underset{Z}{\overset{|}{C}} \diagup$$

Step (1) involves transfer of hydrogen ion to the alkene to form a carbonium ion.

Step (2) is the union of the carbonium ion with base: z.

Step (1) is the difficult step and controls the rate of the reaction. This step involves attack by an acidic electron - seeking reagent that is an electrophillic reagent and hence is called electrophillic addition

(ii) Nucleophilic addition reactions:

These reactions are brought about by nucleophiles. The characteristics reaction of aldehyde and ketone are nucleophilic addition reaction i.e., base catalysed addition of HCN to aldehydes or ketones.

$HO^- + HCN \rightarrow H_2O + CN^-$

Conjugation of electron withdrawing groups activate the carbon-carbon multiple bonds towards nucleophillic addition.

The substituents reduce the p electron density, thereby aid the attack of the nucleophile and stabilize the carbanion formed on attack by delocalization of the negative charge

Polar functional groups Eg $>C = 0$, CN, $>C=N$, $>C=S$ etc., also undergo nucleophillic addition.

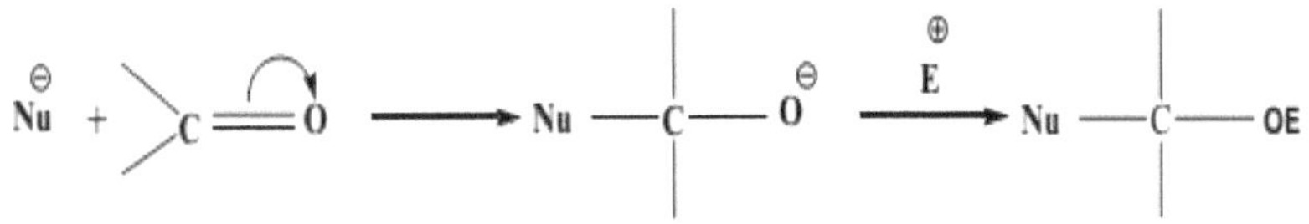

Nucleophilic addition to carbonyl group, therefore a characteristic reaction of aldehyde and ketones.Considering the steric and electronic factors (inductive effect) of the group attached to the carbonyl, carbon, the reactivity of the carbonyl groups decreases in the order:-

$$H_2C = O \quad > \quad RCHO \quad > \quad R_2CO \quad > \quad ArCHO \quad > \quad Ar_2CO$$

(iii) Free radical addition reactions:

Addition reactions brought about by free radicals are called free radical addition reactions for example addition of HBr to alkenes in presence of peroxides.

$$CH_3-CH=CH_2+HBr \xrightarrow{\text{Peroxide}} \underset{\text{n-propyl hydride}}{CH_3-CH_2-CH_2Br}$$

The reaction proceeds through following mechanism.

$$R-O-O-R \xrightarrow{\Delta} 2RO°$$

$$RO· + HBr \rightarrow ROH + Br·$$

$$CH_3\text{—}CH\text{=}CH_2 + Br \xrightarrow{\text{slow}} CH3\text{—}\cdot CH\text{—}CH_2\text{—}Br$$

$$CH3\text{—}\cdot CH\text{—}CH2\text{—}Br \xrightarrow[\text{fast}]{\text{HBr}} CH_3\text{—}CH_2CH_2\text{—}Br + Br$$

$$Br\cdot + Br\cdot \longrightarrow Br_2$$

REARRANGEMENT REACTION

These reactions involve the migration of an atom or a group of atoms from one atom to another within the same molecule.

Some reactions involving rearrangement.

$$CH_3-CH_2-CH_2-CH_2-Br \xrightarrow[575K]{AlCl_3} \underset{Br}{CH_3-CH_2-\overset{|}{C}H-CH_3}$$

$$\underset{CH_3}{\overset{CH_3}{CH_3-\overset{|}{\underset{|}{C}}-CH_2-Br}} \xrightarrow{C_2H_5OH} \underset{OCH_2CH_3}{\overset{CH_3}{CH_3-\overset{|}{\underset{|}{C}}-CH_2-CH_3}}$$

$$\underset{CH_3}{\overset{CH_3Br}{CH_3-\overset{|}{\underset{|}{C}}-CH_2}} \xrightarrow{Alc.KOH} \underset{CH_3}{\overset{CH_3}{CH_3-\overset{|}{C}=C-CH_3}}$$

$$\underset{H}{\overset{CH_3}{CH_3-\overset{|}{\underset{|}{C}}-CH=CH_2}} \xrightarrow{HCl} \underset{Cl}{\overset{CH_3}{CH_3-\overset{|}{\underset{|}{C}}-CH_2-CH_3}}$$

$$R-\overset{\overset{O}{\|}}{C}-NH_2 \xrightarrow{\quad Br_2/KOH \quad} R-NH_2 + K_2CO_3$$

1° amide   1° amine

1, 2 Hydride shift

1, 2 Methyl shift

REVIEWS OF ALKYL HALIDE REACTIONS

	Methyl, 1°	2°	3°	Regio-chemistry	Stereo-chemistry
SN$_2$	Strong nucleophile	Strong nucleophile	Never	-	Inversion of configuration
SN$_1$	Never	Weak nucleo-phile	Weak nucleo-phile	allylic resonance forms and carbocation arrangements	Racemic mixture
E$_2$	E$_2$, only if using a base that is strong base and non-nucle-ophile (SNN)	E$_2$, only if using a base that is strong base and non-nucleo-phile (SNN)	Any strong base	Satzeff product produced in most cases	Antiperiplanar is required for −X and the β −H (trans alkene if possible)
E$_1$	Never	Weak base	Weak base	Satzeff product favour always	Trans alkene formed
SN$_2$ /E$_2$	Methyl halide cannot eliminate, 1o halide favors SN$_2$ unless using SNN base	Mixture can occur if strong base is also a strong nucleophile	SN$_2$ cannot occur E$_2$ product only	-	-

SN_1 /E_1	Never	Mixture always, unless no β-H present	Mixture always, unless no β-H present	-	-

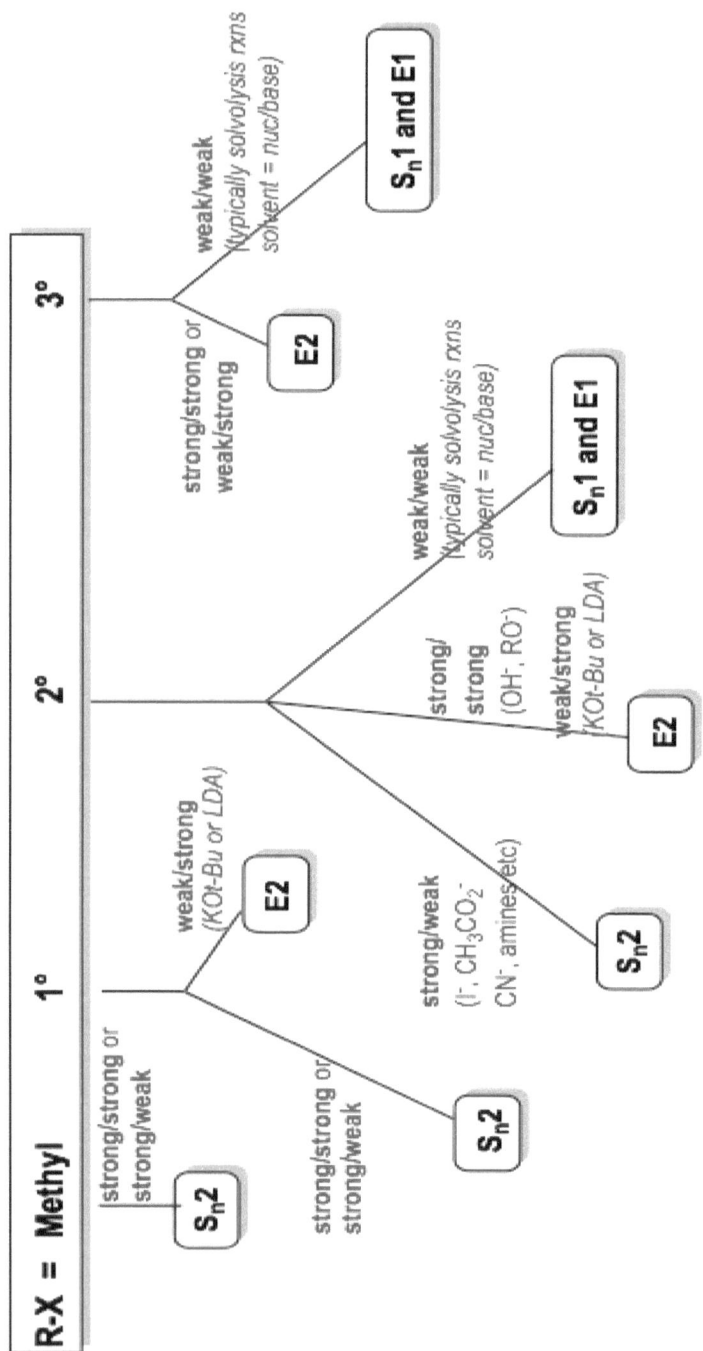

SN₁ or SN₂ Reactions:

A Guide to Deciding Which Reaction is Occurring

STEP 1: The structure of the substrate

☞ **Remember**: the structure of the substrate is a very important consideration in determining if a reaction occurs by an Sn1 or Sn2 mechanism.

☞ What is the structure of the substrate?

   Determine this.

☞ Remember the trend of substrate reactivity for SN_1 & SN_2:
   o **SN_1**: $3° > 2° > 1° >$ methyl
   o **SN_2**: methyl $> 1° > 2° > 3°$

☞ If your substrate is tertiary ($3°$): **SN_1 highly favored.** It won't go by SN_2.

☞ If your substrate is secondary ($2°$): Not the best substrate for SN_1, but it still is ok. Not the best for Sn2 also, but it could still go by this mechanism. In other words, it could go either way, so you must look at other factors before making your decision.

☞ If your substrate is primary ($1°$): **SN_2 favored.** It won't go by SN_1.

☞ If your substrate is methyl: **SN_2 highly favored.** It won't go by SN_1.

STEP 2: The nature of the nucleophile

☞ Is the nucleophile strong or weak? (alternate: good or bad).

☞ SN_2 reactions favor strong nucleophiles.

☞ SN_1 reactions favor weak nucleophiles.

☞ What makes a nucleophile strong?

  o <u>Negative charge:</u>

  ▪ A negatively charged species is a better nucleophile than a similar, uncharged species. In particular, a base is a stronger nucleophile than its conjugate acid.

  o <u>Electronegativity:</u>

  ▪ Nucleophilicity decreases from right to left on the periodic table, following the increase in electronegativity.

  o <u>Size and Polarizability:</u>

  ▪ Nucleophilicity increases down a group on the periodic table, following the increase in size and polarizability.

☞ **What makes a nucleophile weak?**

  o Neutral charge

☞ **Remember sterics!**

  ▪ Bulky nucleophiles slow down reaction rates

STEP 3: Nature of the leaving group

☞ Sn1 and Sn2 reactions favor good leaving groups. Therefore, this aspect really not a major factor in deciding if a reaction follows a SN_1 or SN_2 mechanism.

☞ **HOWEVER: the nature of the leaving group plays an important role in determining if a reaction will undergo a substitution reaction at all!**

☞ **What is a good leaving group?**

  o Electron withdrawing, to polarize the carbon atom on the substrate

  o stable (not a strong base) once it has left

  o polarizable (able to stabilize the transition state)

☞ Weak bases that are common, good leaving groups:

  o Cl^- , Br^-, I^-

  o Sulfonate, sulfate, phosphate (see your notes)

  o neutral molecules:

    ☞ H_2O

    ☞ Alcohols (R-OH)

    ☞ Amines (R_3N)

    ☞ Phosphines (R_3P)

☞ **The following are never leaving groups:**

  o Hydroxide (OH^-)

  o Alkoxide (RO^-), like $CH_3CH_2O^-$

  o Amide (NH_2^-)

STEP 4: The nature of the solvent

☞ Solvent does play a role in determining whether a reaction goes by a SN_1 or SN_2 mechanism. However, it is typically not a major role...but it can "tip the scales" in the favor of one mechanism depending on the nature of the nucleophile and the substrate.

☞ **Polar protic solvents:**
  o Have acidic hydrogens
  o Very strong solvating power
  o Very good for SN_1 reactions.
  o Examples: water, alcohols

☞ Polar aprotic solvents:
  o Do not have acidic hydrogens
  o Good solvating power, but not as strong as polar protic solvents.
  o Very good for SN_2 reactions.
  o Examples: acetone, acetonitrile, dimethylformamide, crown ethers

☞ Aprotic solvents:
  o Non-polar solvents.
  o Not good for either SN_1 or SN_2.
  o Problem: nucleophiles not typically soluble in these solvents. Therefore, they are not really useful for substitution reactions.

Worked examples:

a)

$$CH_3CH_2\overset{\displaystyle CH_3}{\underset{\displaystyle H}{\overset{|}{\underset{|}{C}}}}\!\!-\!\!Cl \quad + \quad CH_3OH \quad \xrightarrow{CH_3OH}$$

Analysis:

1) Substrate: secondary. Can go either SN_1 or SN_2

2) Nucleophile: Weak nucleophile (it's neutral).

3) Solvent: polar protic. Good for SN_1.

4) Leaving group: Cl, which is a good leaving group.

Decision:

Remember that substrate structure and the nucleophile play major roles in this decision. The substrate is secondary, which can go either SN_1 or SN_2. Therefore, you must consider other factors. The nucleophile is weak, which is good for SN_1. The solvent is polar protic, which is also good for SN_1. The leaving group is good, which doesn't really matter here, but it does indicate that a substitution reaction (whichever mechanism) will occur.

Answer: SN_1 mechanism.

b) $CH_3CH_2CH_2CH-NH_2$ + NaOH $\xrightarrow{\text{acetone}}$

Analysis:

1) Substrate: primary. Good for SN_2.

2) Nucleophile: OH^-, Strong nucleophile, good for SN_2.

3) Solvent: polar aprotic. Good for SN_2.

4) Leaving group: NH_2^-, **which is an extremely bad leaving group.**

Decision:

Everything points to a SN_2 mechanism until the leaving group is considered. In this case, the leaving group is very poor. Therefore, it is doubtful if this reaction will even work at all.

Answer: No reaction.

c)

$$CH_3CH_2CH_2CH_2CH_2-I \quad + \quad NaOCH_3 \quad \xrightarrow{\quad CH_3CN \quad}$$

Analysis:

1) Substrate: primary. Good for SN_2.

2) Nucleophile: OCH_3^-, Strong nucleophile, good for SN_2.

3) Solvent: polar aprotic. Good for SN_2.

4) Leaving group: I^-, a very good leaving group.

Decision:

Classic example of an SN_2 reaction. Everything points to it.

Answer: SN_2 reaction.

CH_3OH

Analysis:

1) Substrate: primary. Good for SN_2

2) Nucleophile: I⁻, Strong nucleophile, good for SN_2.

3) Solvent: polar protic. Good for SN_1, not the best for SN_2.

4) Leaving group: Br⁻, a very good leaving group.

Decision:

The data suggests SN_2, except for the solvent. Methanol is a polar protic solvent, which is good for a SN_1 reaction. However, given the nature of the substrate and nucleophile (both good for SN_2), the solvent won't be that important.

Answer: SN_2 reaction.

The keys to deciding the mechanism(s) is to classify the reactivities of the two reactants.

   1) Classify the alkyl halide (R-X) as either:

methyl, 1°, 2°, or 3°

2) Classify the nucleophile/base as either a strong or weak nucleophile, strong or weak base, and a bulky or not bulky base. Since nucleophilicity and basicity trends are related, there are only four possible combinations.

a) strong nucleophile and strong base

b) weak (bulky) nucleophile and strong base

c) strong nucleophile and weak base

d) weak nucleophile and weak base

Use the flowchart or table below to decide which mechanism or combination of mechanisms will be operative.

R-X =

Nuc/Base Strength	methyl	1°	2°	3°
strong/strong	SN2	SN2	E2	E2
strong/weak	SN2	SN2	SN2	no reaction
weak/strong	no reaction	E2	E2	E2
weak/weak	no reaction	no reaction	SN1/E1	SN1/E1

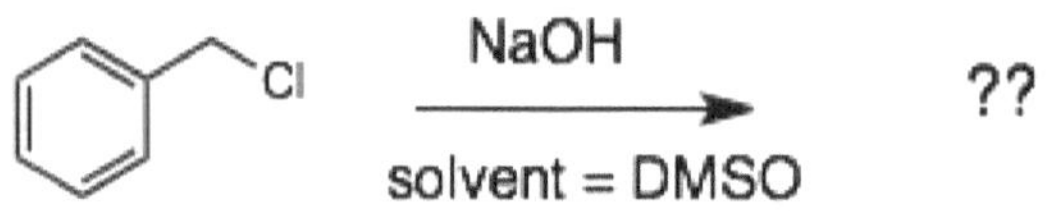

NaOH

solvent = DMSO

??

analysis:

R-X = 1°

-OH = strong nuc

strong base

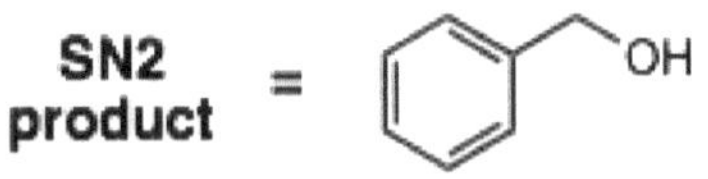
SN2
product
=
OH

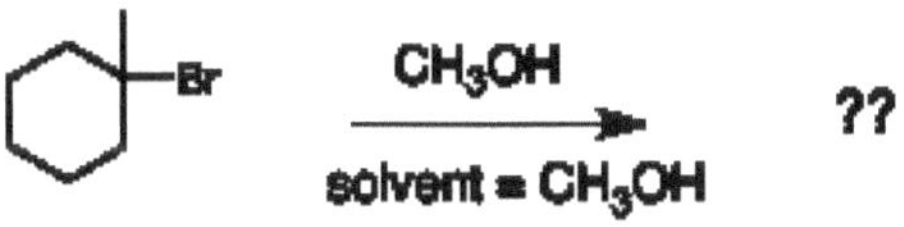
Br
CH3OH
solvent = CH3OH
??

Analysis

R-X = 3°

CH3OH = weak nucleophile

weak base

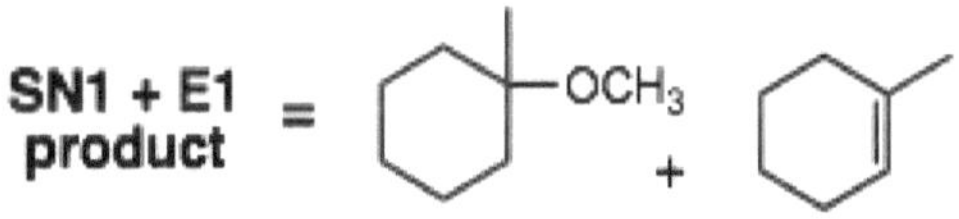
SN1 + E1
product
=
OCH3
+

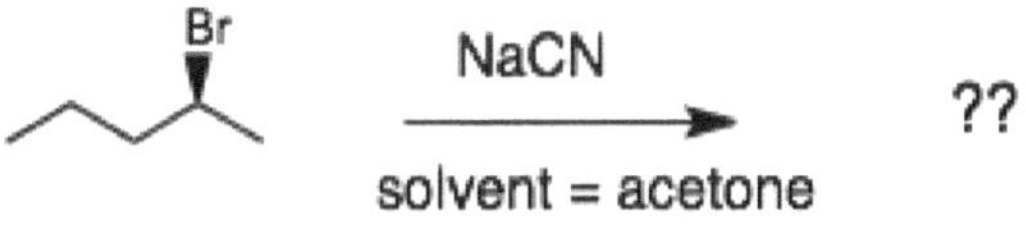
Br
NaCN
solvent = acetone
??

Analysis

R-X = 2°

-CN = strong nucleophile

weak base

SN2 product =

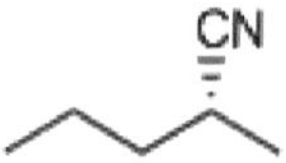

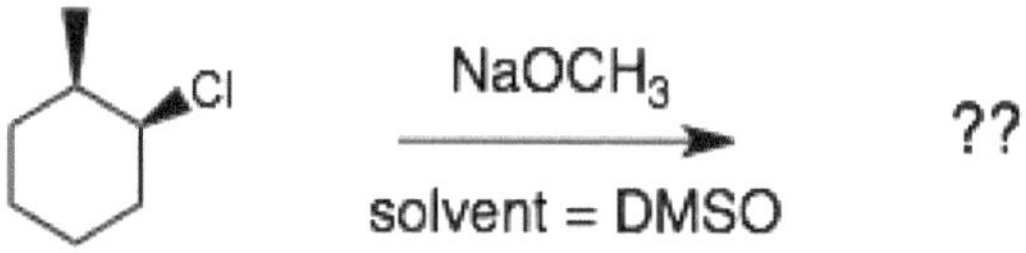

SN2 product structure with CN group

NaOCH₃

solvent = DMSO

??

Analysis

R-X = 2°

-OCH3 = strong nucleophile

strong base

E2 products =

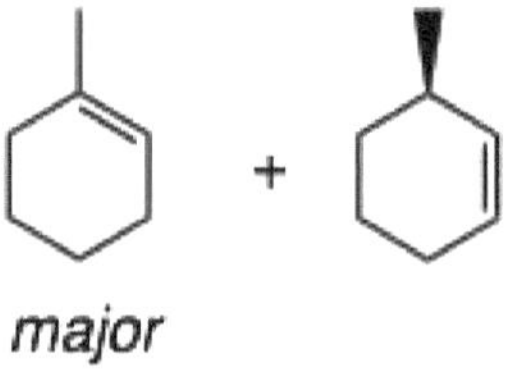

+

major

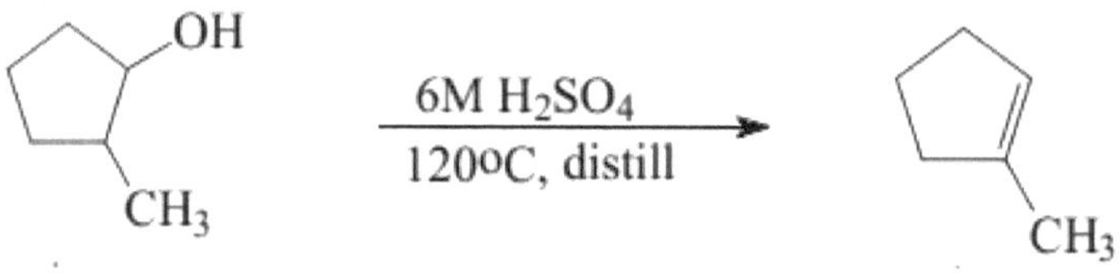

6M H₂SO₄

120°C, distill

E1

KOC(CH₃)₃

in (CH₃)₃COH

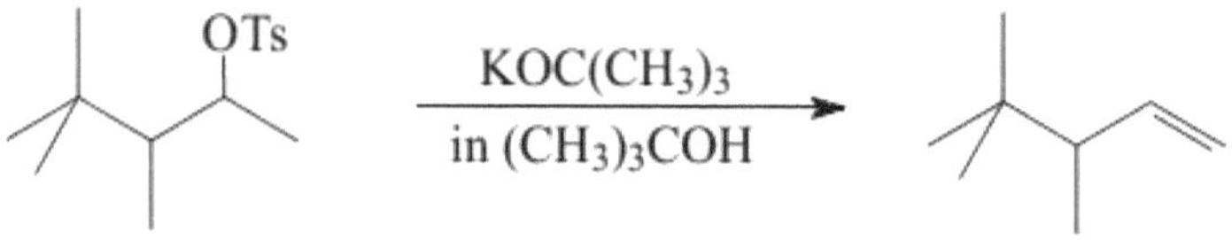

E2

SN1

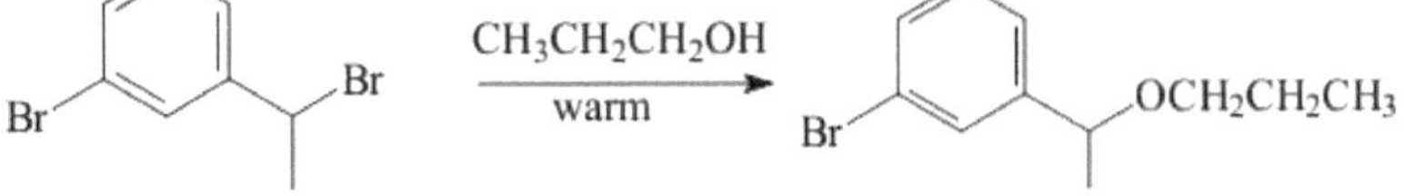

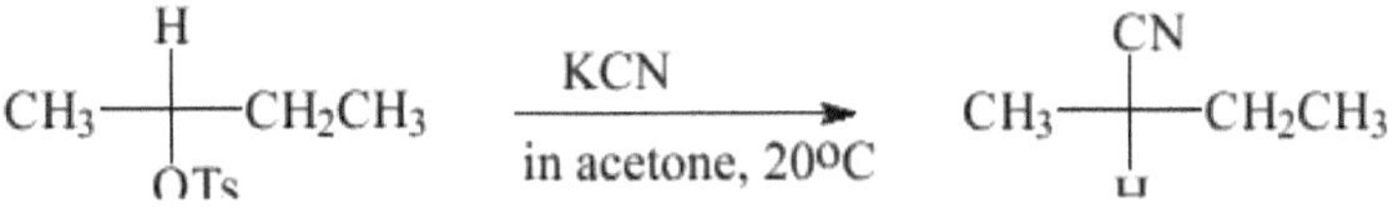

3-bromo compound + CH₃CH₂CH₂OH (warm) → ether product

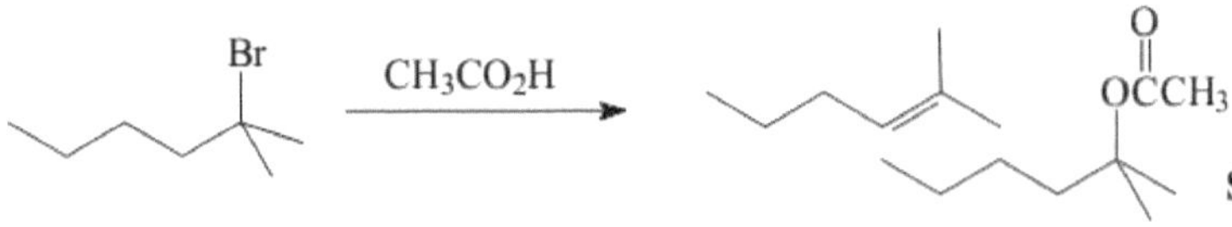

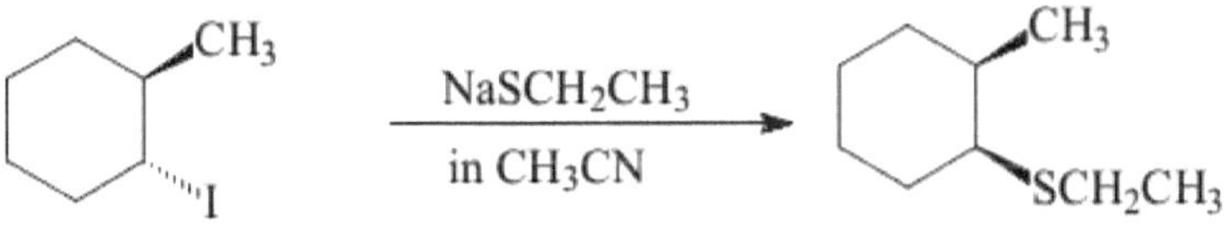

$$CH_3CH_2CH_2OH$$
warm

SN2

$$CH_3-\overset{H}{\underset{OTs}{|}}-CH_2CH_3 \xrightarrow[\text{in acetone, 20}^oC]{KCN} CH_3-\overset{CN}{\underset{\text{LI}}{|}}-CH_2CH_3$$

E1

$$CH_3CO_2H$$

SN1

SN2

$$NaSCH_2CH_3$$
in CH₃CN

$$CH_3CH_2CH_2CH_2CH_2Cl \xrightarrow[\text{in methanol, room temp.}]{NaOCH_3} CH_3CH_2CH_2CH_2CH_2OCH_3$$

SN2

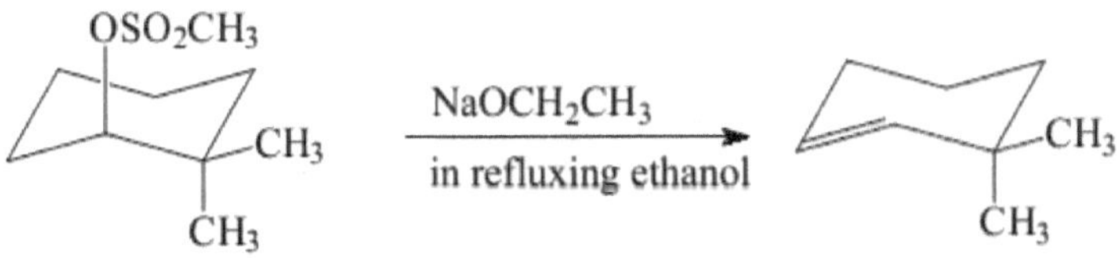

$$NaOCH_2CH_3$$
in refluxing ethanol

E2

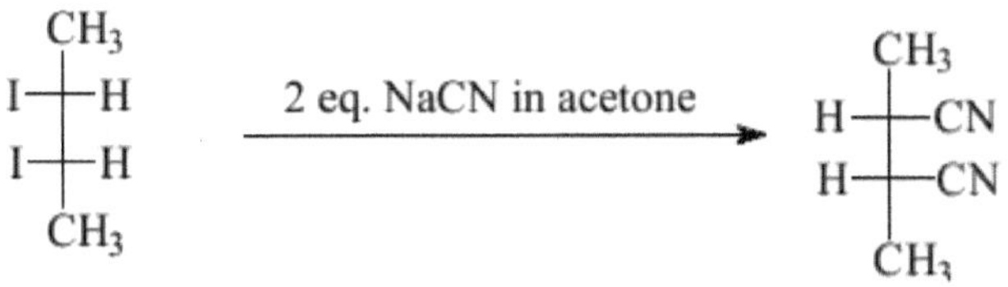

$$\begin{array}{c} CH_3 \\ I-\!\!-H \\ I-\!\!-H \\ CH_3 \end{array} \xrightarrow{\text{2 eq. NaCN in acetone}} \begin{array}{c} CH_3 \\ H-\!\!-CN \\ H-\!\!-CN \\ CH_3 \end{array} \quad \textbf{SN2}$$

Cl–cyclohexane with CH₃ → $CH_3CH_2CH_2OH$, warm → product with OCH₂CH₂CH₃ and CH₃, **SN1**

CH_3Cl → $NaNH_2$ in ammonia → H_2NCH_3 **SN2**

cyclopentane with CH₃ and OH → 85% H_2SO_4, 110°C → cyclopentene with CH₃ **E1**

structure with Br → CH_3CH_2OH with $AgNO_3$ room temp. → product with CH_3CH_2O **SN1**

structure with I → $KOC(CH_3)_3$ in $(CH_3)_3COH / \Delta$ → alkene product **E2** Hofmann

CH_3····cyclohexane····Br → $NaSCH_3$ in DMSO → CH_3····cyclohexane····SCH_3 **SN2**

benzene-CH_2OMs → $NaOCH_3$ in methanol, heat at reflux → benzene-CH_2OCH_3 **SN2**

CHAPTER 6

AROMATICITY

Aromaticity can now be defined as the ability to sustain an induced ring current. A compound withthis ability is called diatropic.There are several methods of determining whether a compound can sustain a ring current, but the most important one is based on NMR chemical shifts. In order to understand this, it is necessary to remember that, as a general rule, the value of the chemical shift of a proton in NMR spectrum depends on the electron density of its bond, the greater the density of the electron cloud surrounding or partially surrounding a proton, the more up field is its chemical shift.This rule has several exceptions; one is for proton in the vicinity of an aromatic ring. When an external magnetic field is impulsed upon an aromatic ring the closed loop of aromatic electrons circulates in a diamagnetic ring current, which sends out a field of its own.As can be seen in the diagram, this induced field curves around and in the area of the proton is parallel to the external field, so that the field feltby the aromatic proton is greater than it would have been in the absence of the diamagnetic r ing current. The protons are moved downfield compared to where they would be if electron density were the only factor. The ordinary olefinic hydrogens are found at 5 to 6 δ , while the hydrogens of benzene rings are located at about 7 to 8 δ.

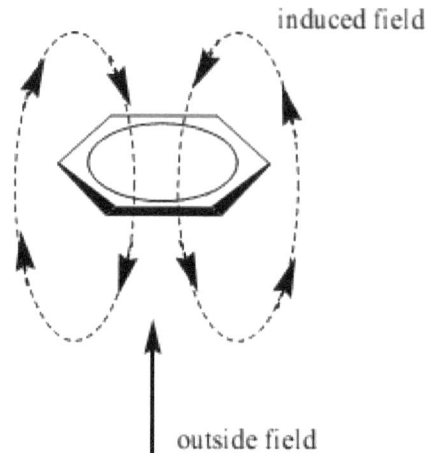

If the proton attached to the ring are shifted downfield from the normal olefinic region, we can conclude that the molecule is diatropic and hence aromatic. In addition, if the compound is diatropic, these will be shifted up field. This method cannot be applied to compounds that have no protons in either category e.g. the dianion of squaric acid.

CONDITIONS FOR AROMATICITY

For a compound to be aromatic one looks for diamagnetic ring current, equal or

approximately equal bond distances, planarity, chemical stability and the ability to undergo

aromatic substitution.

1. The structure must be cyclic.

2. The ring must be planar.

3. Each of the rings must be SP2 hybridized (or occasionally SP hybridized) and have an unhybridized p- orbital.

4. The total number of p electrons in the molecule or ion should be (4n+2) n where n+0, 1, 2, 3…........

5. The unhybridized p- orbital must overlap to give a continuous ring of parallel orbital (the condition of planarity is for effective overlap).

6. This delocalization of p electrons over the ring result in the lowering of the electronic energy

HUCKEL (4n+2) RULE FOR AROMATICITY

Huckel carried out molecular orbital calculation on monocyclic systems CnHn containing a pi electrons and each carbon atom providing one pi electrons and as a result connected aromatic stability (high delocalization energy or high resonance energy) with the presence of (4n+ 2)pi electrons in a closed shell.

To be aromatic, a molecule must have 2(n=0), 6(n=1), 10(n=2)…....... pi electrons. In this description of aromaticity, no mention is made of the number of carbon atom in the ring; the essential requirement is the presence of (4n+2)pi electrons.

Another requirement, for Aromaticity is planarity of the ring. If the ring is not planar, overlap of the p- orbital is diminished or absent. Thus if a molecule is a monocyclic planar system and contains (4n+2)pi electrons that molecule will exhibit aromatic character (i.e.) will have unusual stability. For benzene ring or shell of six pi electrons (i.e.) bonding molecular orbital are doubly filled.

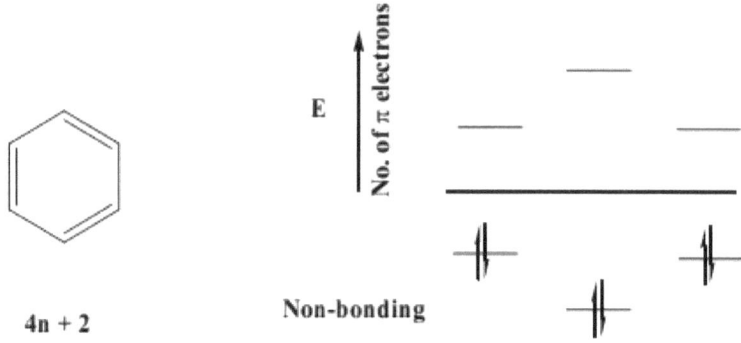

4n + 2

Determining Aromaticity

To determine if a molecule is aromatic, investigate its structure for the qualifiers. If all are present within the molecule, then it is aromatic.

Criteria for Aromaticity:

Conjugated : there needs to one "p" orbital from each atom in the ring, so each atom must be either sp^2 or sp hybridised.

Cyclic : linear systems are not aromatic, all atoms in the ring must be involved in the π system (i.e. no sp^3 atoms)

Planar : if the ring is planar flat then this means there is good overlap interaction between the "p" orbitals....not always easy to consider.

The Huckel Rule..... (4n+2) π electrons in the cyclic conjugated π system (n = 0, 1, 2, 3 etc.) This is equivalent to an odd number of π-

electrons pairs).

In order for a compound to be aromatic, all FOUR of these criteria must be met.

Exercises

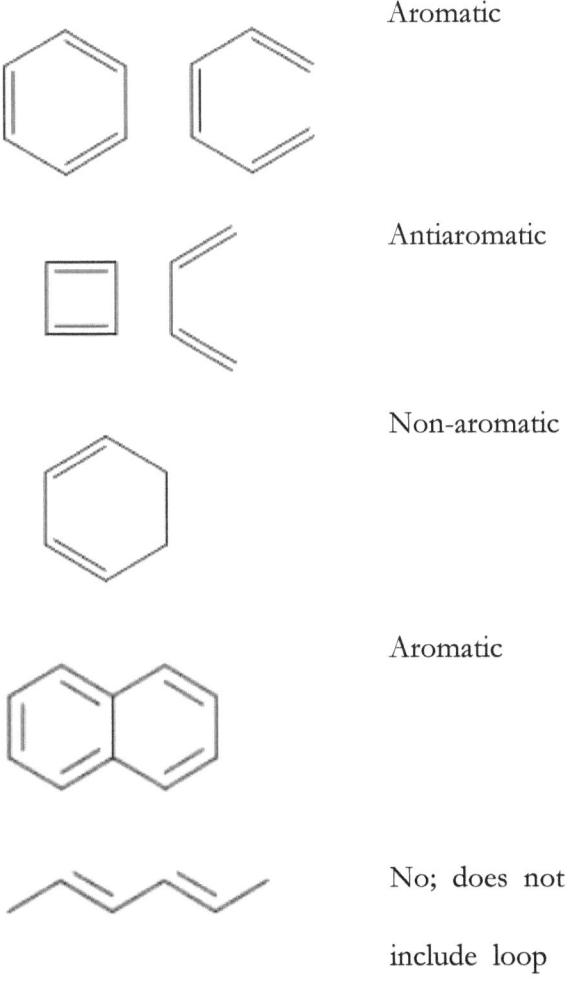

Aromatic

Antiaromatic

Non-aromatic

Aromatic

No; does not

include loop

of overlapping p orbitals

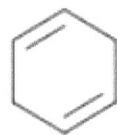

No; does not

include loop

of overlapping p orbitals

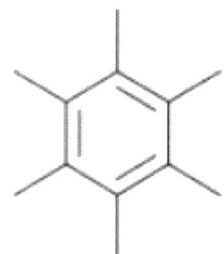

Aromatic

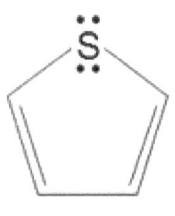

Aromatic - only 1 of S's lone pairs counts as π electrons, so there are 6 π electrons, n=1

Not aromatic - not fully conjugated, top C is sp³ hybridized

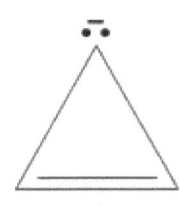

Not aromatic - top C is sp²
hybridized, but there are 4 π
electrons, n=1/2

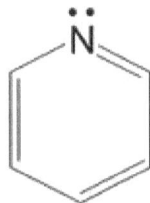

Aromatic - N is using its 1 p orbital
for the electrons in the double
bond, so its lone pair of electrons
are not π electrons, there are 6 π
electrons, n=1

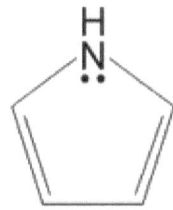

Aromatic - there are 6 π electrons,
n=1

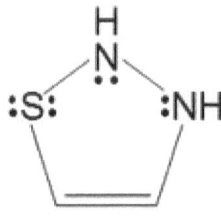

Not aromatic - all atoms are sp²
hybridized, but only 1 of S's lone
pairs counts as π electrons, so
there 8 π electrons, n=1.5

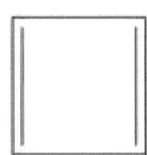

Not aromatic - there are 4 π
electrons, n=1/2

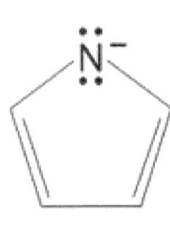

Aromatic - only 1 of N's lone pairs counts as π electrons, so there are 6 π electrons, n=1

Not aromatic - not fully conjugated, top C is sp³ hybridized

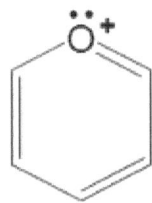

Aromatic - O is using its 1 p orbital for the elections in the double bond, so its lone pair of electrons are not π electrons, there are 6 π electrons, n=1

Aromatic

2Pi Aromatic

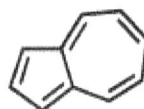

10 pi, Aromatic

8pi, not aromatic

Conjugation and Aromaticity

Conjugation requires at least three overlapping p orbitals in t he same plane so that electrons can be delocalized for better stability. Aromaticity cannot exist without conjugation because aromatic molecules require planarity and overlapping p orbitals.

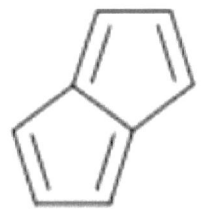

Step 1: Does the molecule have conjugation

Yes, the atoms are all planar with

more than three overlapping p

Orbitals

Step2 Is the molecule aromatic?

Pi bonds are present within a cyc lic structure

Each atom has a p orbital, formi ng a loop

P orbitals overlap and lie in the

same plane

Violates Hückel's Rule

$(4n+2 = 8; n = 6/4)$

Not aromatic

Conclusion: The molecule has conjugation, but is no aromatic.

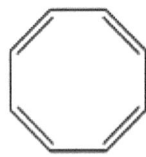

Not conjugated (the molecule has a tub shape and the C=C are perpendicular); Not

aromatic – violates Hückel's rule

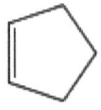

Not conjugated – does not contain at least three atoms with planar p orbitals; Not

aromatic –
   does not contain closed loop of planar, overlapping p orbitals

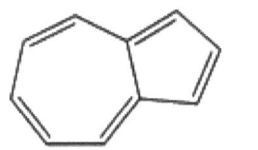

Conjugated; Aromatic –
   meets all criteria

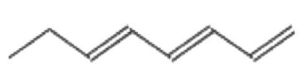

Conjugated, Not aromatic –
   does not contain closed loop of planar, overlapping p orbitals

Conjugated; Aromatic –
meets all criteria

Conjugated; Aromatic –
meets all criteria

Resonance and Aromaticity

Resonance exists as a result of electron delocalization in a molecule. Different patterns emerge as a result of structure and atom arrangement within a molecule. Resonance provides an extra stability due to electron delocalization, and consequently; aromatic rings have resonance structures due to cycling double bonds. Aromatic molecules must have resonance; however,

not all molecules with resonant structures are aromatic

Determine if the molecule below has resonance, aromaticity, both, or neither

Step 1: Does the molecule have resonance?

The pi bonds in the molecule can switch places, a property seen in alkene rings, resulting in a resonance hybrid:

Step 2: Is the molecule aromatic?

Yes, the atoms are all planar with more than
three overlapping p orbitals Pi bonds are present within a cy clic structure. Each atom has a p orbital, forming a loop

The p orbitals overlap and lie in same plane

Satisfies Hückel's Rule (4n+2 = 14; n = 3)

Aromatic

Conclusion: The molecule has resonance, and is aromatic.

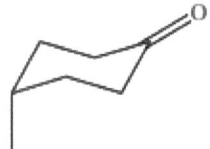

No resonance; No aromaticity

$CH_3CH_2CH_2NH_2$ No resonance; No Aromaticity

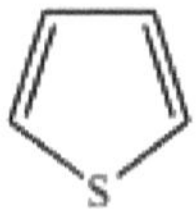

Resonance; Aromaticity

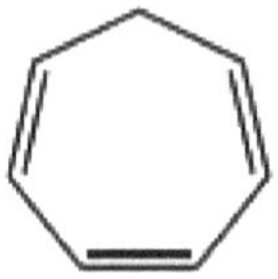

Resonance; No Aromaticity

Nonaromatic

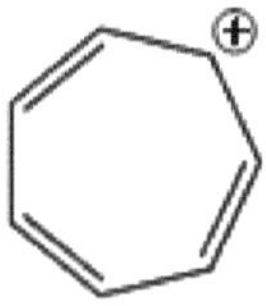

Resonance; Aromaticity

Resonance; No aromaticity

Annulenes

Completely conjugated monocyclic hydrocarbons are called annulenes.

Examples,

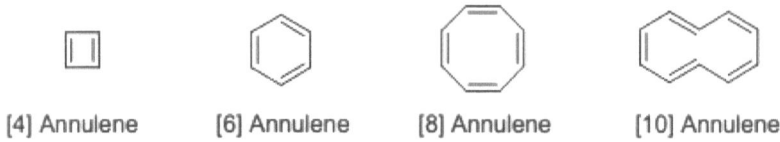

The criteria for aromaticity that we discussed earlier can be applied to higher annulenes as well. However, achieving planarity is a hurdle for many larger rings due to potential steric clashes or angle strains. If the ring (with 4n+2 πelectrons) is sufficiently large such that planarity does not cause steric or angle strains,the system would adopt that conformation, get stabilization through electron delocalization and become aromatic. Larger annulenes with 4n πelectrons are not antiaromatic because they are flexible enough to become non-planar and become non-aromatic.

[10]-Annulene

[10]-Annulene would be aromatic as it has (4n+2) but it is a nonaromatic compound. [10]-Annulene that has only *cis* double bonds cannot have the planar conformation because of angle strain. [10]-Annulene that has two *trans* double bonds cannot adopt a planar conformation either, because two hydrogen atoms interfere with each other.

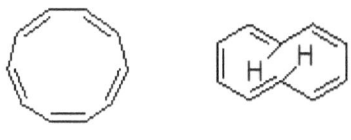

[10]-Annulene

[12]-annulene

[12]-annulene (4n, n = 3) is antiaromatic and hence is not stable above -50oC. Its dianion (4n+2, n = 3) is however stable up to 30o C and is aromatic

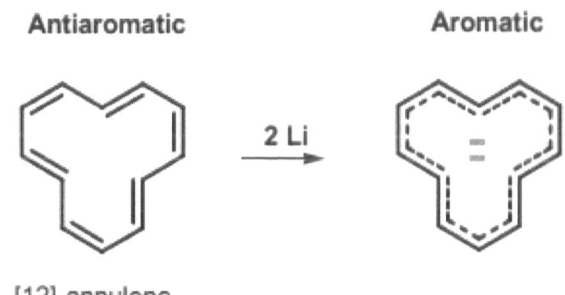

[12]-annulene

[16]-annulene

[16]-annulene shows significant bond alteration, characteristic of a polyene structure (C-C, 1.46Ao; C−C, 1.34 Ao). It is nonplanar and is nonaromatic. Its dianion has been prepared and shows aromatic character (4n+2 system).

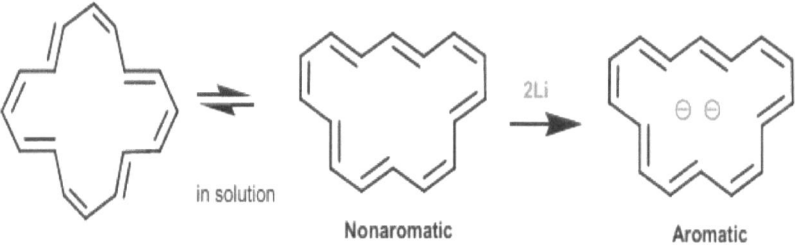

in solution

Nonaromatic   Aromatic

Some larger annulenes with (4n+2) π-electrons such as [14]-annulene and [18]-annulene can achieve planar conformations to have aromatic properties.

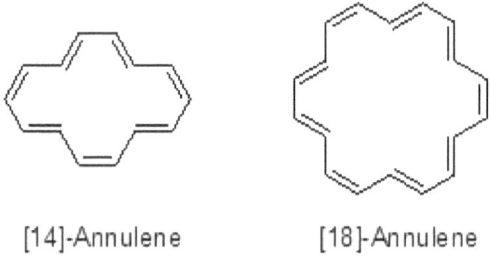

[14]-Annulene   [18]-Annulene

Cyclopropene is not aromatic because one of its ring atoms is sp^3 hybridized so it does not fulfill the criterion for aromaticity. But the cyclopropenyl cation is aromatic because it has an uninterrupted ring of *p*-orbital and (4n+2) π-system. The cyclopropenyl anion is antiaromatic as it has (4n) π-system.

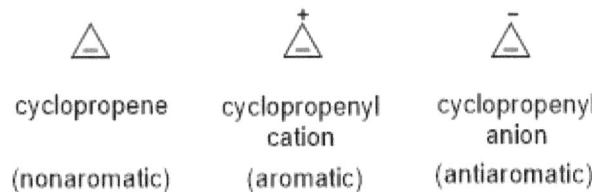

cyclopropene	cyclopropenyl cation	cyclopropenyl anion
(nonaromatic)	(aromatic)	(antiaromatic)

Cyclopentadiene is not aromatic because of the presence of sp^3 hybridized carbon atom. The cyclopentadienyl anion is aromatic because it has an uninterrupted ring of p-orbital and (4n+2) π-system. The cyclopentadienyl cation is antiaromatic as it has (4n) π-system.

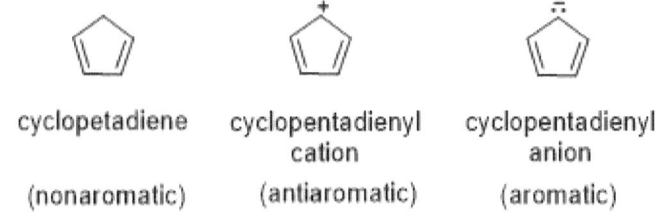

cyclopetadiene	cyclopentadienyl cation	cyclopentadienyl anion
(nonaromatic)	(antiaromatic)	(aromatic)

Cycloheptatrienyl cation and cyclooctatetraene dianion are aromatic compounds because they have uninterrupted ring of p-orbital and (4n+2) π-system.

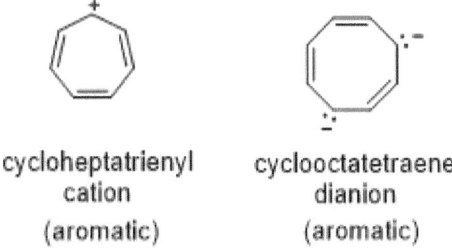

cycloheptatrienyl cation	cyclooctatetraene dianion
(aromatic)	(aromatic)

Cyclopropenone and cycloheptatrienone are stable aromatic compounds. We know that the double bond in carbonyl (C=O) group is polarized to give partial positive charge on the carbon atom and partial negative charge on the oxygen atom. So cyclopropenone and cycloheptatrienone are considered to be aromatic as it obeys (4n+2) π-rule. But the same reason makes cyclopentadienone to be antiaromatic and it is unstable, rapidly undergoes a Diels-Alder dimerization.

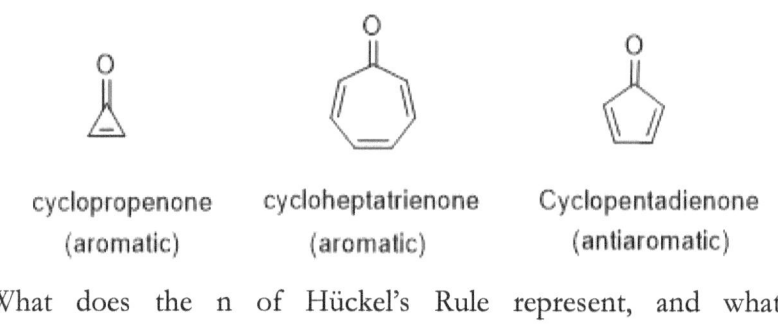

| cyclopropenone | cycloheptatrienone | Cyclopentadienone |
| (aromatic) | (aromatic) | (antiaromatic) |

What does the n of Hückel's Rule represent, and what does it mean if it is an integer or not an integer?

The "n" of Hückel's Rule is simply an indicator of aromatici ty. It does not "stand for" a certain word, but is instead us ed as a calculator. If "n" is a whole number integer, the m olecule can be aromatic, and if "n" is a fraction or non-integ er, the molecule is not aromatic.

Comparing Aromaticity, Antiaromaticity and Non-aromaticity

	Aromatic	Antiaromatic	Non-aromatic
• Cyclic	Yes	Yes	Will fail at least one of these
• Has completely conjugated system of p orbitals in ring of molecule	Yes	Yes	
• Planar	Yes	Yes	
• π electrons in the system	4n+2 (i.e., 2, 6, 10, …)	4n (4, 8, 12, …)	N/A